Nelson Thornes **Framework English**

Skills in **Non-Fiction**

Geoff Reilly
and **Wendy Wren**

Series Consultant:
John Jackman

Nelson Thornes

Contents

Arthur
Ignatious.

Here are several extracts from biographies of the author Arthur Conan Doyle.

Arthur Ignatious Conan Doyle was born on May 22, 1895 in Edinburgh. His father, Charles Altamont Doyle, was a chronic alcoholic and often indulged in erratic behaviour. There was little spare money during Arthur's childhood because of his father's excesses.

Some members of the Doyle family, however, were wealthy and paid for Arthur's studies from the age of nine. He spent seven years at school in England. Discipline at the school was strict and it is thought that his only moments of happiness occurred when he wrote to his mother or played cricket.

After leaving school, Arthur went to the University of Edinburgh to study medicine. It was here he met Dr Joseph Bell on whom Arthur based his most famous character, Sherlock Holmes.

At the age of 22 Charles Altamont Doyle married Mary Foley. She was 17 and a vivacious and very well educated young lady. She had a passion for books and was a master story teller. Arthur wrote in his autobiography, 'In my early childhood, as far as I can remember anything at all, the vivid stories she would tell me stand out so clearly that they obscure the real facts of my life'.

His father's excessive drinking kept the family relatively poor and caused a strong bond to form between Arthur and his mother. While he was away in England at school, he wrote to her regularly, a habit that lasted for the rest of her life. It was at school he realised he, too, had the gift of story telling.

On returning home at the age of 17, one of the first things he did was to co-sign the committal papers of his father which consigned him to a lunatic asylum.

Arthur Conan Doyle became a medical student after leaving the Jesuit school in England. He studied at the University of Edinburgh and met some future authors, such as James Barrie and Robert Louis Stevenson. He also met Dr Joseph Bell, one of his teachers, who is said to have impressed Arthur with his qualities of observation, logic, deduction and diagnosis.

He was two years into his studies when he tried his hand at writing a short story which was called *The Mystery of Sasassa Valley*.

After obtaining his Bachelor of Medicine and Master of Surgeon's degree, he gained employment as the medical officer on the steamer, *Mayuba*, which went between Liverpool and the west coast of Africa.

Arthur Conan Doyle's writing career began while he was at university. His first short story, *The Mystery of Sasassa Valley*, was published in an Edinburgh magazine called *Chamber's Journal*. His second story, *The American Tale*, was published in *London Society*.

After a position as the medical officer on the *Mayuba* and a stint with an unscrupulous doctor in Plymouth, Doyle went to Portsmouth to open his own practice. He then divided his time between his medical work and trying to become a recognised author.

In March 1866, Doyle began work on a story which was to make him a household name. *A Study In Scarlet* was published in *Beeton's Christmas Annual* in 1868 and introduced us to Sherlock Holmes and Dr Watson. Two years later *The Sign of Four*, a full length novel featuring the great detective, established Doyle as one of the most popular novelists of his day.

TEXT LEVEL WORK

Comprehension

A 1 What was:

a Arthur Conan Doyle's father's full name?
b his mother's maiden name?

2 What did Arthur enjoy doing at school?

3 What 'gift' did Arthur discover he had inherited from his mother?

4 Where did Arthur study medicine?

5 In which story did Sherlock Holmes first appear?

B 1 Explain the following in your own words:

'... *indulged in erratic behaviour* ...'
'... *tried his hand* ...'
'... *a household name* ...'.

2 What impression do you get of Arthur's life at school?

3 What evidence in the extracts is there to show that Arthur and his mother had a close relationship?

4 Do you think Arthur was more interested in being a doctor or a writer? Explain your reasons.

C Skim the biographical extracts and make notes on anything to do with Doyle's writing career.

WORD LEVEL WORK

Vocabulary

Dictionary and contextual work

Use a dictionary and the context of the passage to explain the meanings of these words:

1 chronic	5 autobiography	9 logic
2 erratic	6 obscure	10 deduction
3 excesses	7 bond	11 diagnosis
4 vivacious	8 consigned	12 established

Spelling

'wh' words

Key words: **wh**en **wh**ile **wh**ich

1 Use these key words in sentences of your own.

2 Learn these important 'wh' words:

mean**wh**ile **wh**y **wh**ere **wh**at

whenever **wh**ereas **wh**ether

SENTENCE LEVEL WORK

Grammar and punctuation

Nouns – collective and abstract

> Remember, a noun is a word that names something.
> There are different types of noun:
>
> *Collective nouns* name collections of people or animals, eg
>
>   A flock of sheep
>
> The word 'flock' is a collective noun for a group of sheep.
>
> *Abstract nouns* refer to things that cannot be touched, eg
>
>   childhood   justice   soul

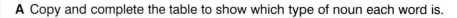

A Copy and complete the table to show which type of noun each word is.

Noun	Collective	Abstract
herd		
faith		
peace		
flock		
truth		
colony		
talent		
friendship		
tribe		
pack		

B Copy and complete the table, inserting the correct abstract noun made from each of the adjectives. The first one is done for you.

Adjective	Abstract noun
strong	strength
cowardly	
courageous	
thirsty	
hungry	
scarce	
beautiful	
free	
anxious	
hysterical	

TEXT LEVEL WORK

Writing

Research

> When you research a subject you need to use various sources, make notes and write up your notes in paragraphs.
>
> The biographical extracts on Arthur Conan Doyle are the sources of information you could use to write a brief biography of the author.

Language features
Chronology
Most biographies present information about the subject in chronological order, eg

> *'Arthur Ignatious Doyle was born on May 22, 1895 ...'*
> *'... from the age of nine ...'*
> *'After leaving school ...'.*

Factual information
Biographies present the facts of the subject's life, eg

> *'At the age of 22, Charles Altamont Doyle married Mary Foley ...'*
> *'In March, 1866, Doyle began work on a novel ...'.*

Opinion
Often a biographer has to form an opinion of the subject but has no concrete facts. This is signalled by such phrases as, eg

> *'... it is thought that ...'*
> *'... it is said that ...'.*

Writing assignment
The information in the four extracts can be put together to form a more complete biography of Arthur Conan Doyle.
Follow these stages:

1 Make notes on Doyle's:

- life at home
- life at school
- life at Edinburgh University
- his writing career.

You may find the information for each set of notes in more than one extract.

2 Write up your notes in four paragraphs, ie

- his home life
- his school life
- his university life
- his writing career.

Work only from your notes and do not copy from the original extracts.

> *"Miscarriages of justice are a blot on a civilised society."*

Return of death penalty rejected

MPs deliver decisive verdict on move to bring back hanging.
Stephen Goodwin reports

As MPs debated the return of the death penalty for the 14th time since its suspension in 1965, Michael Howard, the Home Secretary, warned of the "irreparable damage" to the criminal justice system had innocent people been executed.

"Miscarriages of justice are a blot on a civilised society," said Mr Howard, who until three years ago had favoured the death penalty for the murder of police or prison officers and for murder with firearms or explosives.

"To spend years in prison for a crime you did not commit is both a terrible thing and one for which release from prison and financial compensation cannot make amends. But even this injustice cannot be compared with the icy comfort of a posthumous pardon."

Mr Howard was speaking during a Committee Stage debate on the Criminal Justice and Public Order Bill. John Greenway, Conservative MP for Ryedale and a former Metropolitan police officer, moved a new clause to make the murder of a police officer punishable by death, which was rejected by 383 votes to 186, a majority of 197.

A second clause, moved by Elizabeth Peacock, Tory MP for Batley and Spen, to reintroduce the death penalty for all murders, but subject to confirmation by the Court of Appeal, was also rejected by 403 votes to 159, a majority of 244.

Mr Greenway, whose eldest son and prospective daughter-in-law are police officers, said there was "something particularly outrageous and despicable" about the murder of a police officer.

In the three years since MPs last debated the death penalty for police murder – and rejected it by 185 votes to 135 – eight officers had been murdered, the most recent only two weeks ago.

"If the life of just one of those eight officers had been spared by the death sentence, wouldn't this sanction have been justified?" Mr Greenway asked. "I take the view that these evil men who show such utter contempt for the lives of serving police officers deserve to pay for their horrific crimes by forfeiting their own lives." He said it was an incontrovertible fact that when Britain had the death penalty it was extremely rare for criminals engaged in serious robberies to be armed with guns or knives lest in the heat of the moment a member of the gang panicked and committed murder. "I believe that the threat of the death penalty would have a similar effect on some criminals today."

Intervening, Sir Nicholas Fairbairn, a former Conservative solicitor general for Scotland, said he had appeared in 17 capital cases. He did not believe the death penalty had a deterrent effect on offenders and said it could have "a really bad effect" on counsel. "If I make a mistake in asking the wrong questions ... the man may go to the trap. Therefore, I believe it is wrong and evil in every way."

Mrs Peacock recalled her warning in the last hanging debate that it was time MPs came down from their ivory tower and did what the British people wanted them to do – support the reintroduction of the death penalty.

"My postbag suggests that nothing has changed. In fact there is more and more support throughout the country for this action. To me, beating an old lady to death in her own home or killing a policeman on duty are equally abhorrent – they are both murder. In my view, in a proven case of murder, it would be the duty of the court to pass the death penalty."

However, she noted that many murders were "carried out in domestic circumstances" and said that under her new clause death sentences would immediately be referred to the Court of Appeal to decide whether the circumstances justified the substitution of life imprisonment.

Menzies Campbell QC, Liberal Democrat MP for Fife NE, said the cases of the Guildford Four and the Birmingham Six showed how mistakes could be made.

"Some, or indeed all of them, might well have suffered the same fate as Timothy Evans. If they had, then they would simply have underlined the dangerous finality of the cruel and inhuman punishment which capital punishment represents. Are we so confident of ourselves and our judicial system that we are willing to wager the life of any system on capital punishment?"

Mr Howard explained that it was the failure of the appeal system in the case of the Birmingham Six that, three years ago, had led him to re-examine his support for capital punishment. "We should not fail to consider the irreparable damage which would be inflicted on the criminal justice system in this country had innocent people been executed," he said.

The shadow Home Secretary, Tony Blair, told the house he opposed the two proposed death penalty clauses on moral and utilitarian grounds. "The most powerful argument is the risk that we will kill the innocent," he declared.

Murdering a police officer was heinous, he said, "but so are terrorist killings of blowing people up in pubs, young girls raped then brutally murdered – and in all these circumstances the death penalty, if appropriate in one, would be appropriate in all."

Seamus Mallon (SDLP Newry and Armagh) said: "If we do incorporate the taking of life, the killing of people, into our legislation, then we have taken the values and the methods of the terrorist, of the gangster, of the gunman, and written it into out legislation.

The Independent

> *"The most powerful argument is the risk that we will kill the innocent"*

TEXT LEVEL WORK

Comprehension

A 1 When was the death penalty '*suspended*'?

2 For what four categories of murder did Mr Howard once support the death penalty?

3 According to Mrs Peacock, on which side of the debate are the British people?

4 What, according to Mr Howard, is the '*irreparable damage*' that could be inflicted on the criminal justice system?

5 What position did Tony Blair have at the time of this debate?

B 1 What effect do you think the headline has on the reader?

2 Explain the following in your own words:

a '*financial compensation*'
b '*subject to confirmation*'
c '*their ivory tower*'.

3 For what three reasons do you think Mr Greenaway supports the death penalty for the murder of a police officer?

4 Explain in your own words: '*... the death penalty had a deterrent on offenders ...*'.

5 What '*fate*' do you think Timothy Evans '*suffered*'?

C Read the report carefully and make notes on:

a the arguments for bringing back the death penalty
b the arguments against bringing back the death penalty.

Quote the evidence you find in support of your notes.

WORD LEVEL WORK

Vocabulary

Dictionary and contextual work

Use a dictionary and the context of the passage to explain the meanings of the following words:

1 suspension	7 sanction
2 irreparable	8 contempt
3 miscarriages	9 forfeiting
4 posthumous	10 incontrovertible
5 confirmation	11 abhorrent
6 prospective	12 utilitarian

Spelling

Soft 'c'

Key words: justi**c**e inno**c**ent offi**c**er soli**c**itor

1 Use these key words in sentences of your own.

2 Learn these important soft 'c' words:

    de**c**ide   eviden**c**e   ne**c**essary   introdu**c**e

    conton**c**e   re**c**ent   **c**ircumstan**c**es

SENTENCE LEVEL WORK

Grammar and punctuation

Irregular nouns – singular and plural

Some nouns that end in 'f' or 'fe' are changed to 'ves' in the plural, eg

    cal**f** ⟶ cal**ves**

Some old English plurals are still in use, eg

    child ⟶ children

Some nouns ending in 'o' take 's' as the plural, while others take 'es', eg

    Studi**o** ⟶ studi**os**   tomat**o** ⟶ tomat**oes**

We just add 's':

- for words ending in 'oo', eg cuck**oo** ⟶ cuckoo**s**
- for musical words, eg cell**o** ⟶ cello**s**
- for abbreviations, eg photo ⟶ photo**s**

Nouns ending in 'ex' or 'ix', change the ending to 'ic' and add 'es', eg

    ind**ex** ⟶ ind**ices**   matr**ix** ⟶ matr**ices**

Copy and complete the table. Check your answers in a dictionary.

Singular	Plural
knife	
ox	
kangaroo	
echo	
appendix	
cod	
gallows	
buffalo	
piano	
matrix	

TEXT LEVEL WORK

Writing
Reporting

> *Return of death penalty rejected* is a written report of a debate. Arguments for and against the death penalty were put forward and then a vote was taken. The written report of what happened appeared in a newspaper.

Language features

Headline

The report has a short headline which is designed to attract the reader's attention. There are several examples of alliteration, eg

> 'Return ... rejected'
>
> '... deliver decisive ...'
>
> 'bring back'.

Organisation

The first few paragraphs of the report give the reader a summary of the main points of the debate:

- what was debated:

  'As MPs debated the return of the death penalty ...'

- the main speakers:

  '... said Mr Howard'

  'John Greenaway ... moved a new clause ...'

  'A second clause, moved by Elizabeth Peacock ...'

- the outcome:

  '... rejected by 383 votes to 186 ...'

  '... also rejected by 403 votes to 150 ...'.

The rest of the report goes into greater detail of the arguments for and against, eg

> 'If the life of just one of those eight officers had been spared by the death penalty ...'
>
> 'He did not believe the death penalty had a deterrent effect ...'
>
> '... what the British people wanted them to do ...'.

Factual information

The writer provides the reader with information necessary to understand what was being debated and who was taking part, eg

> '... its suspension in 1965 ...'
>
> '... John Greenaway, Conservative MP for Ryedale and former Metropolitan police officer ...'
>
> 'In the three years since MPs last debated the death penalty ... eight officers had been murdered ...'.

Opinions

In debates, as well as factual information, opinions are put forward, eg

'Therefore, I believe it is wrong and evil in every way.'

'In my view, in a proven case of murder ...'.

Quotations

The report quotes the actual words spoken by those involved in the debate, eg

'... the most powerful argument is the risk that we will kill the innocent'

'... If we do incorporate the taking of life, the killing of people, into our legislation ...'.

Reported speech

The writer also uses reported speech to summarise some of the points that were made, eg

'He said that it was an incontrovertible fact that ...'

'... said he had appeared in 17 capital cases ...'.

Writing assignment

Imagine a debate has taken place on whether it should be made illegal to ride a bicycle without a helmet. Write a report of that debate for a newspaper.

Planning

- Come up with a snappy, attention-grabbing headline.
- Make notes on the arguments for and against.
- Invent the names of three of four 'characters' who spoke in the debate.
- Draft what each one said.

The report

Write a brief summary of what was debated and what the outcome was. Include both:

- quotes and reported speech to show the arguments for and against
- factual information and the opinions of the speakers.

Hamlet on screen.

Hamlet is Shakespeare's most famous and most often filmed play ... and the reason? In the words of Daniel Rosenthal in his book *Shakespeare on Screen*, it is obvious:

'Hamlet is a rattling good story, a supernatural revenge thriller whose hero's hesitancy generates unique tension: not a 'whodunnit? but a 'why-doesn't-he-do-it?'

From Laurence Olivier's 1948 film through to Ethan Hawke in the 2000 version, *Hamlet* has been filmed many times. It has been shortened and filmed in its entirety; played in Elizabethan and modern costume; and enacted in historical and contemporary settings.

Here is some information about famous screen versions of the play.

1 1948   UK production   153 mins   B/W

Cast:

Hamlet: Laurence Olivier	Polonius: Felix Aylmer
Gertrude: Eileen Herlie	Laertes: Terence Morgan
Claudius: Basil Sydney	Horatio: Norman Wooland
Ophelia: Jean Symonds	

Produced by Laurence Olivier   Directed by Laurence Olivier

Critics' verdict:

'The greatness of the Olivier *Hamlet* is that he has made it a movie for everybody. Be you 9 or 90, a PhD or just plain Joe, *Hamlet* is the movie of the year.'
Washington Post

'... in its subtlety, vividness and control, Olivier's performance is one of the most beautiful ever put on film.'
Time

Academy Awards for Best Picture and Best Actor

2 1990   US production   135 mins   Colour

Cast:

Hamlet: Mel Gibson	Polonius: Ian Holm
Gertrude: Glenn Close	Laertes: Nathaniel Parker
Claudius: Alan Bates	Horatio: Stephen Dillane
Ophelia: Helena Bonham Carter	Ghost: Paul Scofield

Produced by Dyson Lovell   Directed by Franco Zeffirelli

Critics' verdict:

'... strong, intelligent and safely beyond ridicule'
The New York Times

'He blunders into the poetry as though it were awkwardly placed furniture.'
Mail on Sunday

3 1996 US/UK production 243 mins Colour

Cast:

Hamlet: Kenneth Branagh	Polonius: Richard Briers
Gertrude: Julie Christie	Laertes: Michael Maloney
Claudius: Derek Jacobi	Horatio: Nicholas Farrell
Ophelia: Kate Winslet	Ghost: Brian Blessed

Produced by David Barron   Directed by Kenneth Branagh

Critics' verdict:

'... To die, to sleep through half the movie.'
   The New York Post

'Branagh hasn't brought length at the cost of longuers, and that's an achievement.'
   Evening Standard

TEXT LEVEL WORK

Comprehension

A 1 Who produced and directed the 1948 version of *Hamlet*?

2 Which character is mentioned in two of the versions but not in the third?

3 In which year was the film starring Mel Gibson produced?

4 What part did Richard Briers play in the 1996 version?

5 Which of the three versions is the longest?

B 1 Explain the following in your own words:

   a '... *unique tension* ...'
   b '... *in its entirety* ...'
   c '... *contemporary settings* ...'.

2 Why do you think the 1996 film was 90 minutes longer than the 1948 film?

3 About which film were the critics totally positive in their reviews?

4 Which two versions had mixed reviews?

C Which of the three versions of *Hamlet* would you be most interested in seeing? Take into account:

• the date of production
• the cast
• the critics' views

and explain your reasons.

WORD LEVEL WORK

Vocabulary and dictionary work

Use a dictionary and the context of the information passage to explain the meaning of these words:

1 rattling	5 enacted	9 blunders
2 supernatural	6 PhD	10 longuers
3 hesitancy	7 subtlety	
4 generates	8 ridicule	

Spelling

'ful' endings
Key word: beauti**ful**

1 Use this key word in a sentence of your own
2 Learn these important 'ful' words:

peace**ful**	skil**ful**	wonder**ful**
aw**ful**	thought**ful**	success**ful**

> *HINT*
> *The only '**full**' that ends in a double 'l' is '**full**'!*

SENTENCE LEVEL WORK

Grammar and punctuation

Adjectives – comparative and superlative

Remember. Adjectives are sometimes used to compare the description of two or more people, animals, things or places.
There are five rules to form the *comparative* and *superlative* forms of regular adjectives.

1 Short adjectives of one syllable add 'er' and 'est' to the adjective, eg

   Adjective = old: Comparative = old**er**: Superlative = old**est**.

2 Adjectives ending in 'y', change this letter to 'i' and add 'er' and 'est', eg

   Adjective = eas**y**: Comparative = eas**ier**: Superlative = eas**iest**.

3 Adjectives ending in 'e', take off the 'e' and add 'er' and 'est', eg

   Adjective = larg**e**: Comparative = larg**er**: Superlative = larg**est**.

4 Adjectives ending in a vowel plus a consonant, double the consonant and then add 'er' and 'est', eg

   Adjective = b**ig**: Comparative = b**igger**: Superlative = b**iggest**.

5 Adjectives with three or more syllables and some adjectives of two syllables do not change. Instead, 'more' and 'most' are put in front of them, eg

   Adjective = beautiful: Comparative = **more** beautiful: Superlative = **most** beautiful.

A Copy and complete comparative and superlative for each word in the table.
Then, put in the number of the rule for each word.
The first one has been done for you.

Rule	Adjective	Comparative	Superlative
Rule 1	young	younger	youngest
	heavy		
	humorous		
	wise		
	delicious		
	brave		
	careful		
	famous		
	fat		
	few		
	busy		
	hot		

B Copy and complete the table, stating which rule is correct for each comparative or superlative adjective from *Hamlet*.

Adjectives	Comparative/Superlative	Rule
more removèd ground		
whose lightest word		
most unnatural murder		
most foul, strange and unnatural		
duller shouldst thou be		

TEXT LEVEL WORK

Writing

Reviews

After the 'first night' of a play or the premier of a film, reviews appear in newspapers. They are written by critics who give their opinion on what they have seen. In the information given about the three film versions of *Hamlet*, quotes from reviews have been included.

Language features

Factual information

A reviewer will either:

- begin the review with a chart or table giving factual information about the film. This will include such things as ...
  - the title, eg *Hamlet*
  - the cast, eg Polonious – Felix Aylmer
  - director/producer, eg Laurence Olivier
  - running time, eg 135 mins

- refer to these pieces of factual information throughout the review.

Opinion

The comments made by a critic about a film are a personal opinion and critics often differ in their opinion, eg

'... *strong, intelligent and safely beyond ridicule ...*'

'*He blunders into poetry as though it were awkwardly placed furniture.*'

Emotive language

Critics rarely use 'ordinary' plain language. A film isn't just 'good' or 'bad' – it is:

wonderful/inspiring/a triumph
or
terrible/embarrassingly awful/a disaster.

For example, Oliver's performance is '*most beautiful*', and Mel Gibson '*blunders*'.

Writing assignment

Imagine a new film of *Hamlet* has just been premiered.

1 Write an information piece which gives:

- the year
- where the film was produced
- the running time
- the cast list (use the names of actors and actresses you have seen in other films)
- the producer and director (look at the back of videos or DVDs to find these names).

2 Write a review of the film from the viewpoint of a critic who thought it was a 'triumph'.

3 Write a review of the film from the viewpoint of a critic who thought it was a 'disaster'.

4 In each review make comments about:

- the set
- the costumes
- the performance of the actor who played Hamlet
- the wonderful or terrible performance of one other actor/actress.

...thin, faint lines

Mars: the dead planet

One night in 1877, Italian astronomer Giovanni Schiaparelli was peering at Mars from his hilltop observatory. Sketching feverishly each time he turned, blinking from his eyepiece, Schiaparelli was in the middle of the most thorough study of the Martian surface that had ever been made. Among many of the details this dedicated astronomer noted was a prevalence of thin, faint lines which criss-crossed the surface of Mars. He described then as 'channels' or, in his native Italian, *canali*. It wasn't very long before Victorian society was full of fanciful ideas of canal-building civilisations on Mars. After all, Mars had many parallels with Earth. Although it is only half the size of our world, its day lasts only 36 minutes longer than our own. It has white polar caps that, from a distance, appear similar to the Earth's. Its axis, with respect to the Sun, is also similarly tilted, so it has similar seasons to ours, although they last twice as long, as a year on Mars is 687 days. If Venus was seen as our twin, then Mars was our smaller cousin.

When the USA finally turned its rockets on Mars in late 1964, scientists had long suspected that the planet was too cold to sustain life, but Schiaparelli's canals were still scored across every map of the red planet. On 15 July 1965 those maps were about to be redrawn, when *Mariner 4* entered the most critical stage of its mission. After eight long months and hundreds of millions of kilometres, it had a mere 20 minutes to capture the first precious images of Mars as it swooped past 10,000 kilometres above its surface. It performed heroically, grabbing 21 pictures down a narrow strip of the planet from north to south before Mars drifted out of sight.

The rate of data transfer at that time was incredibly slow – eight bits of information per second (today's probes send back information about 10,000 times faster). Pictures were stored on magnetic tape and sent back over the course of the following three weeks. When the first view of another world trickled back to JPL in California, the blurred image of the edge of the Martian globe against the black of space sent a ripple of excitement through the watching scientists and journalists. The relief at receiving something, anything, was tangible and the anticipation grew. The cameras were rolling and they were ready for their close-ups.

But when *Mariner 4* finally delivered, it was a crippling body blow. On frame number seven, the surface finally came into focus and the scientists saw ... craters. No canals, no riverbeds, no valleys or mountains, just craters. A sinking feeling washed over mission control. Mars looked as dull as the Moon. The Earth, an active planet, destroys its craters with volcanic eruptions or shifting tectonic plates, but the presence of so many craters on Mars meant that none of that seemed to have happened. Over the next few days more detailed pictures came back, but they only rubbed salt into the wound: more craters.

In 1969, just a few days after Neil Armstrong had set foot on the Moon, two more American craft flew by Mars. Their story was buried under the headlines of the century. Perhaps it was just as well. *Mariners 6* and *7* pretty much confirmed the findings of the first probe, sending back little more than clearer views of the wretched craters. Among the project scientists there was a feeling of anti-climax, one of the team commenting: 'We've got superb pictures, they're better than we could ever have hoped for a few years ago – but what do they show us? A dull landscape, as dead as a dodo. There's nothing much left to find.'

Towering infernos

The first three glimpses of Mars had done nothing but depress geologists. It didn't make sense that the red planet should be as barren as the Moon. It must have been a hot ball of rock when it first formed. Although smaller than the Earth, it is much bigger than the Moon and some of its internal heat must have seeped out in the form of lava over the few billion years of its existence. Surely something on the surface should show signs of that.

On 13 November 1971 *Mariner 9* slammed on its brakes and settled into a gentle 12-hour orbit some 1,400 kilometres above the surface of Mars. *Mariner 9* was going to stay a while and map the whole planet from pole to pole. But Mars took everyone by surprise: the spacecraft was greeted by a planet-wide dust-storm. The first pictures it beamed back were completely featureless.

The year was nearly over when the dust-storms finally started to settle. As the veil gradually receded, the *Mariner 9* scientists were shocked to see four dark spots peeking up through the dust. They had expected nothing more than the rims of vast craters to break through the shroud, but these dark dots had to be many kilometres high. As the days passed the scientists could hardly believe their eyes. The spots were quite clearly the tops of volcanoes – four of them – any one of which would dwarf the biggest on Earth.

> *"... scientists were shocked to see four dark spots ..."*

The largest volcano corresponded to a bright spot that Earth-based astronomers had seen for years and called Nix Olympica (Snows of Olympus). It was promptly re-named Olympus Mons (Mount Olympus) and immediately took up pole position as the biggest volcano in the Solar System, rising 25 kilometres above the plain surrounding it. The other three volcanoes were only a few kilometres shorter. But incredible though they were, these giants were just the beginning of *Mariner 9*'s revelations. As the dust receded from the planet's middle, it revealed a massive canyon – a 180 kilometre-wide gash across the equator long enough to stretch right across the USA. This enormous system of gorges, in places 7 kilometres deep, was named Valles Marineris (Mariner's Valleys) in honour of the spacecraft that found it. It is the biggest feature on the planet, probably formed when the four volcanoes to its northwest bulged out the crust of Mars and ripped this gaping wound in the side of the planet.

David McNab and James Younger

Main image. An aerial view of part of Mars' 3000 kilometre-wide chasm, Valles Marineris, pieced together from Viking Orbiter images.

Inset image. Mariner 9's first view of Mars in late 1971 shows four spots poking up through the layer of dust. Later images revealed dot A to be the giant volcano Olympus Mons.

TEXT LEVEL WORK

Comprehension

A 1 In 1877, what was Giovanni Schiaparelli '*in the middle of*'?

2 List the similarities between Earth and Mars.

3 Which spacecraft '*captured the first precious images of Mars*'?

4 When scientists finally had pictures of the surface:

    a what did they see?
    b what did they not see?

5 What did *Mariner 9* show scientists?

B 1 Explain the following in your own words:

    a '*sinking feeling*'
    b '*crippling body blow*'
    c '*rubbed salt into the wound*'.

2 In what way do you think an unmanned spacecraft could be described as performing '*heroically*'?

3 Why do you think '*it was just as well*' that the missions to Mars of *Mariner 6* and 7 were overshadowed by the moon landing?

4 Why do you think the photographs of volcano tops were so important to the scientists?

C 1 Find one example of each of the following in the passage:

    a an opinion
    b a fact
    c a statistic
    d a reaction.

2 Copy and complete the chronological table:

Date	Event
1877	
1964	
1969	
1971	

WORD LEVEL WORK

Vocabulary

Dictionary and contextual work

Use a dictionary and the context of the passage to explain the meanings of the following words:

1 feverishly	5 scored	9 barren
2 dedicated	6 tangible	10 internal
3 prevalence	7 confirmed	11 receded
4 sustain	8 anti-climax	12 revelations

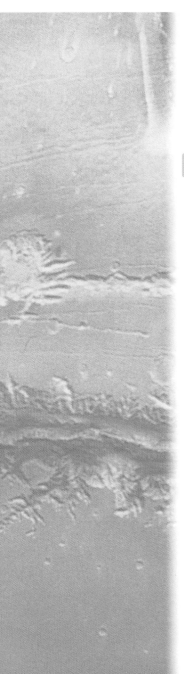

Spelling

'el' words

Key words: channel parallel

1 Use these key words in sentences of your own.

2 Learn these important 'el' words:

pastel easel rebel vessel vowel tunnel novel

SENTENCE LEVEL WORK

Grammar and punctuation

Adjectival clauses

> Remember. A complex sentence is made up of an independent clause and a dependent clause.
>
> The *adjectival clause* is used to modify a noun or a pronoun.
>
> It will begin with a *relative pronoun* ('who', 'whose', 'whom', 'which', and 'that'), eg
>
> > '*The planet was covered by a dust-storm, which surprised everyone.*'
>
> or a *subordinate conjunction* ('when' and 'where'), eg
>
> > '*The year was nearly over when the dust-storms finally started to settle.*'
>
> Those are the only words that can be used to begin an adjectival clause.

A Copy the table. Underline, colour or highlight the adjectival clause in each sentence. Then identify the word that the clause modifies or describes.

Sentence	Word modified
It has white polar caps that appear similar to our own.	
Scientists had long suspected that the planet was too cold to sustain life.	
When the first view of another world trickled back, the blurred image of Mars was exciting.	
It must have been a hot ball of rock when it first formed.	
The spots were quite clearly the tops of volcanoes which would dwarf the biggest on Earth.	

B Join each pair of sentences by replacing the subject of the second sentence, using introductory words eg 'who', 'whose', 'whom', 'which', 'that', 'when' and 'where'.

1 The other three volcanoes were only a few kilometres shorter.
   The volcanoes were just the beginning of *Mariner 9*'s revelations.

2 The dust receded from the planet's middle.
   It revealed a massive canyon.

3 This enormous system of gorges was named Mariner's Valley.
   It is the biggest feature on the planet.

4 The four volcanoes bulged out of the crust of Mars.
   The volcanoes ripped this gaping wound in the side of the planet.

5 Mount Olympus rises 25 kilometres above the plain.
   The volcano is the biggest in the Solar System.

TEXT LEVEL WORK

Writing

Presenting information

> The account of the exploration of Mars is taken from a BBC book which accompanied the series *The Planets* shown on television. It includes a great deal of factual and chronological information but the writer has also given insights into the hopes, expectations, disappointments and elation of those engaged in the study of the planet.

Language features

Factual information
Obviously the writer needs to convey factual information about Mars, eg
> '*... its day lasts only 36 minutes longer than our own ...*'.

Chronology
The writer has presented the stages of that exploration in chronological order so we can follow the 'story' as it unfolded, eg
> '*One night in 1877 ...* '   '*When the USA finally turned its rockets on Mars in 1964 ...*'.

Technical language
As this is a scientific subject, the writer has had to use technical language, eg
> '*The rate of data transfer ... eight bits of information per second ...*'.

Informal style
The writer has used an informal style to capture the human element in the 'story', eg
> '*... sent a ripple of excitement ...*';   '*... they only rubbed salt in the wounds ...*'.

Eyewitness accounts
The writer quotes from those actually involved in the various missions, eg
> '*We've got superb pictures, they're better than we could have hoped for a few years ago – but what do they show us? A dull landscape, as dead as a dodo.*'

Writing assignment
Imagine you are a scientist in a team which has sent *Venutian 1* to explore the planet Venus unsuccessfully, and *Venutian 2*, which successfully sent back pictures and data. Write a report giving factual details but also explaining how you and the team felt throughout the process.

Planning
- research the planet Venus so that your factual information is accurate
- make notes on your thoughts, feelings and reactions throughout the two missions, and those of the other team members.

The report
- write in an 'informal' style to capture and keep your readers' interest
- present the report in chronological order
- include: facts; thoughts; feelings and reactions – quotes from those involved.

Personal choice
Choose one of the following assignments.
Based on the factual detail in the extract:

1 Write a front page newspaper report on the unsuccessful voyage of *Mariner 4* to Mars.
2 Write a front page newspaper report on the successful voyage of *Mariner 9* to Mars.

... we have
a problem

Apollo 13 was launched at 1313 on 11 April 1970. It carried Jim Lovell, Fred Haise and Jack Swigert on a lunar mission. Only fifty-five hours into the flight, disaster struck. A mysterious explosion rocked the ship. Its oxygen and power began draining away. Had the ship been hit by a meteorite? Jim Lovell took a look out of the window ...

... in the hope that whatever problem Odyssey might have would somehow make itself clear. The odds of diagnosing the ship's illness this way were long, but as it turned out, they paid off instantly. As soon as Lovell pressed his nose to the glass, his eye caught a thin, white, gassy cloud surrounding his craft, crystallizing on contact with space, and forming an iridescent halo that extended tenuously for miles in all directions. Lovell drew a breath and began to suspect he might be in deep, deep trouble.

If there's one thing a spacecraft commander doesn't want to see when he looks out his window, it's something venting from his ship. In the same way that airline pilots fear smoke on a wing, space pilots fear venting. Venting can never be dismissed as instrumentation, venting can never be brushed off as ratty data. Venting means that something has breached the integrity of your craft and is slowly, perhaps fatally, bleeding its essence out into space.

Lovell gazed at the growing gas cloud. If the fuel cells hadn't killed his lunar touchdown, this certainly did. In a way, he felt strangely philosophical – risks of the trade, rules of the game, and all that. He knew that his landing on the moon was never a sure thing until the footpads of the LEM had settled into the lunar dust, and now it looked as if they never would. At some point, Lovell understood, he'd mourn this fact, but that time was not now. Now he had to tell Houston – where they were still checking their instrumentation and analysing their readouts – that the answer did not lie in the data but in a growing cloud surrounding the ailing ship.

'It looks to me,' Lovell told the ground uninflectedly, 'that we are venting something.' Then, for impact, and perhaps to persuade himself, he repeated: 'We are venting something into space.'

'Roger,' Lousma responded in the mandatory matter-of-factness of Capcom, 'we copy your venting.'

'It's a gas of some sort,' Lovell said.

'Can you tell us anything about it? Where is it coming from?'

'It's coming out of window one right now, Jack.' Lovell answered, offering only as much detail as his limited vantage point provided.

The understated report from the spacecraft tore through the control room like a bullet.

'Crew think they're venting something,' Lousma said to the loop at large.

'I hear that,' Kranz said.

'Copy that, Flight?' Lousma asked, just to be sure.

'Rog,' Kranz assured him. 'O.K. everybody, let's think of the kinds of things we'd be venting. GNC, you got anything that looks abnormal on your system?'

'Negative, Flight.'

'How about you, EECOM? You see anything with the instrumentation you've got that could be venting?'

'That's affirmed, Flight,' Liebergot said, thinking, of course, of oxygen tank two. If a tank of gas is suddenly reading empty and a cloud of gas is surrounding a spacecraft, it's a good bet the two are connected, especially if the whole mess had been preceded by a suspicious, ship-shaking bang. 'Let me look at the system as far as venting is concerned,' Liebergot said to Flight.

'O.K., let's start scanning,' Kranz agreed. 'I assume you've called in your backup EECOM to see if we can get some more brain power on this thing.'

'We got one here.'

'Rog.'

The change on the loop and in the room was palpable. No one said anything out loud, no one declared anything officially, but the controllers began to recognize that Apollo 13, which had been launched in triumph just over two days earlier, might have just metamorphosed from a brilliant mission of exploration to one of simple survival. As this realization broke across the room, Kranz came on the loop.

'O.K.,' he began. 'Let's everybody keep cool. Let's make sure we don't do anything that's going to blow out electrical power or cause us to lose fuel cell number two. Let's solve the problem, but let's not make it worse by guessing.'

Lovell, Swigert and Haise could not hear Kranz's speech, but at the moment they didn't need to be told to keep cool. The moon landing was definitely off, but beyond that, they were probably in no imminent danger. As Kranz had pointed out, fuel cell two was fine. As the crew and controllers knew, oxygen tank one was healthy as well. Not for nothing did NASA design its ships with backup system after backup system. A space-craft with one cell and one tank of air might not be fit to take you to Fra Mauro, but it was surely fit to take you back to Earth.

Lovell drifted over to the centre of the command module to get a read on his remaining oxygen tank and see how much of a margin of error it would provide them. If the engineers had planned it right, the crew would arrive back home with a substantial load of O_2 to spare. The commander glanced at the meter and froze: the quantity needle for tank one was well below full and visibly falling. As Lovell watched, almost entranced, he could see it easing downward in an eerie, slow-motion slide.

This discovery, horrifying as it was, explained a lot. Whatever it was that had happened to tank two, that event was over. The tank had gone off line or blown its top or cracked a seam or something, but beyond the very fact of its absence, it has ceased to be a factor in the functioning of the ship. Tank one, however, was still in a slow leak. Its contents were obviously streaming into space, and the force of the leak was no doubt what was responsible for the out-of-control motion of the ship. It was nice to know that when the needle finally reached zero, Odyssey's oscillations would at last disappear. The downside, of course, was that so would its ability to sustain the life of the crew.

Lovell knew Houston would have to be alerted. The change in the pressure was subtle enough that perhaps the controllers hadn't noticed it yet. The best way – the pilot's instinctive way – was to play it down; keep it casual. Hey you guys, notice anything about that other tank? Lovell nudged Swigert, pointed to the tank one meter, then pointed to his microphone. Swigert nodded.

'Jack,' the command module pilot asked quietly, 'are you copying O_2 tank one cryo pressure?'

There was a pause. Maybe Lousma looked at Liebergot's monitor, maybe Liebergot told him off the loop. Maybe he even knew already. 'That's affirmative,' the Capcom said.

As near as Lovell could tell, it would be a while before the ship's endgame would play out. He had no way of calculating the leak rate in the tank, but if the moving needle was any indication, he had a couple of hours at least before the 320 pounds of oxygen were gone. When the tank gasped its last, the only air and electricity left on board would come from the trio of compact batteries and a single, small oxygen tank. These were intended to be used at the very end of the flight, when the command module would be separated from the service module and would still need a few bursts of power and a few puffs of air to see it through reentry. The little tank and the batteries could run for just a couple of hours. Combining this with what was left in the hissing oxygen tank, Odyssey alone could keep the crew alive until sometime between midnight and 3am Houston time. It was now a little after 10pm.

Jim Lovell and Jeffrey Kluger

TEXT LEVEL WORK

Comprehension

A 1 When Lovell looked out of Apollo 13's window, what did he see?

  2 What did Liebergot think the spacecraft was venting?

  3 We are told at one point that '*The commander froze*'. Why was this?

  4 How many hours of oxygen did the crew have left from when Lovell noticed that '*the quantity needle from tank one was well below full and visibly falling*'?

  5 What was the air in the '*small oxygen tank*' intended for?

B 1 Explain the following in your own words:

  a '*paid off instantly*'
  b '*matter-of-factness*'
  c '*understated report*'.

  2 Lovell repeats the information that they are venting something '*perhaps to persuade himself*'. What impression does this give you of his state of mind at that time?

  3 What impression do you get of the sort of man Krantz is?

  4 Why do you think NASA designed its ships with '*backup system after backup system*'?

C Find an example of each of the following in the extract:

- a fact
- an opinion
- a reaction
- a thought or feeling we can only know because Jim Lovell was actually there.

WORD LEVEL WORK

Vocabulary

Dictionary and contextual work
Use a dictionary and the context of the passage to explain the meanings of the following words:

1 lunar	5 venting	9 palpable
2 diagnosing	6 analysing	10 metamorphosed
3 iridescent	7 mandatory	11 imminent
4 tenuously	8 vantage	12 oscillations

Spelling

'ai' words
Key words: p**ai**d   **ai**r   cert**ai**nly   **ai**ling

  1 Use these key words in a sentence of your own.

  2 Learn these important 'ai' words:

det**ai**l   br**ai**n   sust**ai**n   portr**ai**t
curt**ai**n   f**ai**th   tr**ai**tor

SENTENCE LEVEL WORK

Grammar and punctuation

Verbs – present tense

> Remember. The *simple past* is used to talk about a completed action in a time before now, eg
>
> > 'Lovell drew a breath ...'.
>
> How long the action took is not important. The time of that action may be recent or may be long ago.
>
> For regular verbs the simple past is formed by adding 'ed' to the basic word, eg
>
> > talk + ed =talked
> > mow + ed = mowed
> > hatch + ed = hatched
>
> Some verbs are called irregular because they do not follow the regular rule of adding 'ed'. These irregular verbs change their form, when making the past tense, to be, to have, to do, eg
>
> | Infinitive | Present | Past |
> |------------|---------|-------|
> | To be | I am | I was |
> | To have | I have | I had |
> | To do | I do | I did |

Change these sentences from the past tense into a question and a negative. The first one has been done for you.

	Sentence	Form
1	Apollo 13 flew to the moon.	positive
	Apollo 13 did not fly to the moon.	negative
	Did Apollo 13 fly to the moon?	question
2	A mysterious explosion rocked the ship.	
3	Jim Lovell looked out of the window.	
4	His eye caught a thin, white, gassy cloud surrounding his craft.	
5	No one said anything out loud.	
6	As Kranz had pointed out, fuel cell two was fine.	
7	Lovell drifted over to the centre of the command module.	

TEXT LEVEL WORK

Writing

Autobiography

> Jim Lovell is the co-author of the book, from which this passage was taken, and he was the commander of Apollo 13. He does not, however, write the account in the first person as you might expect, which makes it an unusual way of writing an 'autobiography'.

Language features

Third person

Rather than write a straightforward first person account of the Apollo 13 mission, Jim Lovell and his co-author, Jeffrey Klugar have written in the third person as if the whole thing had happened to someone else, eg

> 'As soon as Lovell pressed his nose to the glass ...'
> 'Lovell, Swigert and Haise could not hear Kranz's speech ...'.

One reason the writers could have decided to do this is that the 'action' is happening in two places and Lovell, using the first person, could only have recounted what was happening where he was. In this way, we get a clearer picture of:

- what is happening on the spacecraft, eg
  'It looks to me ... that we are venting something.'
- how the people in Houston are responding, eg
  'The understated report from the spacecraft tore through the control room like a bullet.'

Autobiographical details

Even though the style of the writing is biographical rather than autobiographical, Jim Lovell has included details of his thoughts and feelings that you would expect to find in an autobiography, eg

> 'If there's one thing a spacecraft commander doesn't want to see ...'
> '... he felt strangely philosophical ...'
> '... he'd mourn this fact, but that time was not now ...'.

Viewpoint

As the action is taking place in two different places, the reader sees the series of events from two viewpoints:

- the spacecraft
- Houston.

The writers have moved from one to the other in turn so the reader can see the drama unfold.

Writing assignment

Imagine you are one of two astronauts who have made a successful landing on the moon. You leave your lunar module to gather moon rocks and then return. You go through the procedure to fire the rockets, which will take you off the moon's surface, back to the command module, BUT they don't fire.
Write this series of events in the third person. Remember:

- you were there so you can give the reader an idea of how you were feeling
- you were in contact with Houston all the time so the reader knows how they reacted over the radio and how they reacted when you couldn't hear them.

Personal choice

Choose one of the following assignments:

1 Using the details from the extract, write a diary entry as Jim Lovell. Remember:
  - write in the first person
  - do not include things he could not have known about at the time.

2 Research the Apollo 13 mission and write a report of how the astronauts were brought safely back.

How to explore your CD-Rom

The major feature of *The Sunday Times* magazine on 23 September 2001 was called 'Journey Into Space'. The magazine also included a CD-Rom called 'Window on the Universe'. Here are the instructions.

PC USERS:

1) Insert the Window on the Universe (WOU) CD-Rom in the relevant drive on your computer. It should autorun (where you have enabled autorun for your CD-Rom drive). If the WOU CD-Rom does not autorun, use Windows® Explorer, or your preferred file manager, and select the CD-Rom drive labelled **BNSC_WOU1**, then double-click **wou.exe**. This will run the WOU start screen.

2) In order to run this CD-Rom, you will need to have a browser compatible with Netscape® V4 or Microsoft® Internet Explorer V4 (or later). If you do not already have the following, you will also need to install:
Adobe® Acrobat Reader V5 to use the worksheets that come with the CD-Rom.
RealNetworks® RealPlayer V8 to see the videos and animations on the CD-Rom.
Macromedia® Shockwave V8 to see the menus and play the games.
LizardTech™ MrSID® viewer to view/zoom in to the images.

3) You can install any applications you do not already have by clicking on the Essential Software option and selecting the No (not already installed) button for the relevant application. Although you may be prompted to, it should not be necessary to restart your computer after any of the installations in order to use the WOU CD-Rom. Once you have all the necessary software (and all the options are ticked), click NEXT, which will take you to the **Minimum Specification** page.

4) On the **Minimum Specification** page, check that your PC is suitable and then click on Ready to Go. This will take you to the Sunday Times introduction screen; from here you should read and **accept** the Terms of Use.

5) Having accepted the Terms of Use, you will be presented with the screen pictured below. Click on the relevant button. If you can see the rocket, you will be asked to click on the star (bottom), and then you enter the Guided Tour.

6) To maximise your enjoyment of the WOU CD-Rom, you should take the guided tour. However, you can choose **click here for express entry** or **Page 8: Start WOU**.

7) Keep the CD-Rom in the drive until you have finished looking at the WOU CD-Rom. If you want to come back and look at it later, you do not need to reinstall software.

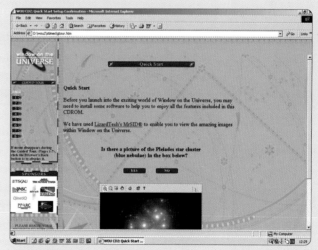

MAC USERS:

1) Insert the Window on the Universe (WOU) CD-Rom in the relevant drive on your computer. It will autorun and bring up a small window – double-click the WOU installer.

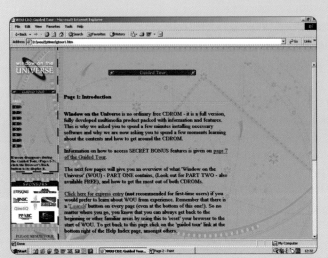

2) In order to run this CD-Rom you will need to have a browser compatible with Netscape® V4 or Microsoft® Internet Explorer V4 (or later). If you do not already have the following, you will also need to install:
Adobe® Acrobat Reader V5 to use the worksheets that come with the CD-Rom.
RealNetworks® RealPlayer V8 to see the videos and animations on the CD-Rom.
Macromedia® Shockwave V8 to see the menus and play the games.

LizardTech™ MrSID® viewer to view/zoom in to the images.

3) The MAC® install process will lead you through screens where you can select the software you need. At the end of the installation, click **Quit**.

4) Double-click the **Launch WOU** icon on your desktop. This will take you to the Sunday Times introduction screen; from here you should read and **accept** the Terms of Use.

5) Once you have accepted the Terms of Use, you will be presented with the screen pictured left. Click on the relevant button. If you can see the rocket, you will be asked to click on the star, and then you enter the Guided Tour.

6) To maximise your enjoyment of the WOU CD-Rom, you should take the guided tour. However, you can choose **click here for express entry** or **Page 8: Start WOU**.

7) Keep the CD-Rom in the drive until you have finished looking at the WOU CD-Rom. If you want to come back and look at it later, you do not need to reinstall software.

THE LAST RESORT: TELEPHONE 020 7711 7900

If you have followed all the instructions and still have problems with the installation process, please ensure before you phone the number above that you have read the readme.txt, the install.txt files, and the relevant help sections on the CD (readme.txt tells you how to do this). In order to receive our technical support, you will need to be near your computer when you call the above number.

TEXT LEVEL WORK

Comprehension

A 1 By what initials is the CD-Rom Window on the Universe referred to throughout the instructions?

2 What browser do you need to have to run this CD-Rom?

3 What software do you need for:
   a the worksheets?
   b the videos?
   c the games?

4 Once you have a rocket on the screen, what must you do to enter the Guided Tour?

5 If you want to look at the CD-Rom again, do you have to reinstall the software?

B 1 Find three examples of imperative verbs.

2 What does the Essential Software option allow you to do on a PC?

3 Why do you not need an Essential Software option on a MAC?

4 Why do you think the information in the box is entitled '*THE LAST RESORT*'?

C Given that this is quite a complicated process, explain why you think these instructions are easy or difficult to follow.

> **HINT**
>
> *Imperative verbs give commands.*

WORD LEVEL WORK

Vocabulary

Dictionary and contextual work
Use a dictionary and the context of the passage to explain the meanings of the following words:

1 insert	5 enabled	9 compatible
2 prompted	6 maximise	10 reinstall
3 relevant	7 preferred	11 animations
4 specification	8 express	12 ensure

Spelling

double 'l' words
Key words: follow   install

1 Use these key words in sentences of your own.

2 Learn these important double 'l' words:

   alliteration   pollution   collect   village
   balloon   shallow   pillow

SENTENCE LEVEL WORK

Grammar and punctuation

Verbs – simple future tense

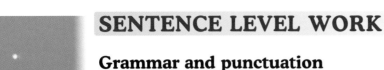

Remember. The *simple future* refers to a time later than now, and expresses facts or certainty. In English, there are many ways of expressing future time. One of the most common is using the modal auxiliary verbs:

> you will/you'll; he will/he'll; she will/she'll; they will/ they'll;
> I shall/I'll; we shall/we'll.

The future tense is used to:

- predict a future event, eg 'It will snow tomorrow.'
- express a spontaneous decision, eg 'I'll buy the tickets by cheque.'
- express willingness, eg 'I'll do the ironing. He'll carry your rucksack.'
- express unwillingness, eg 'I won't leave until I've seen the end of the game.'
- make an offer, eg 'Shall I open the door?'
- make a suggestion, eg 'Shall we go to the cinema on Saturday?'
- ask for advice or instructions, eg 'What shall I tell my parents?'
- give orders, eg 'You will do exactly as I asked.'
- give an invitation, eg 'Will you come clubbing with me?'

Change these simple future sentences into the negative and interrogative (questioning) forms. The first one is done for you.

Sentence	Form
1 You will complete the table.	simple future
You won't complete the table.	negative
Will you complete the table?	interrogative
2 This will run the WOU start screen.	
3 You will need to have a browser compatible with Netscape® v4.	
4 You will also need to install this software.	
5 You will be asked to click on the star.	
6 You will be presented with the screen pictured left.	

TEXT LEVEL WORK

Writing

Instructions

How to explore your CD-Rom is two sets of numbered instructions. As with many instructions concerned with computers, you need to decide which set of instructions are for the type of computer you have.

Language features

Structure

These instructions have to be followed in a particular order and, because of this, are numbered, eg

> '1) Insert the Window on the Universe ...'
> '2) In order to run this CD-Rom ...'.

Imperative verbs

Imperative verbs give orders, eg

> '... **select** the CD-Rom drive ...'
> '... **check** that your PC is suitable ...'.

Sentence types

Instructions do not usually ask questions. They make statements, eg

> 'You can install any applications you do not already have ...'.

Abbreviations

As these are a technical set of instructions, the writer has abbreviated some terms:

- a general term that the reader is likely to know is abbreviated throughout, eg
  - 'CD-Rom'
  - 'PC'
- an unusual term is given in full the first time it is used and then abbreviated, eg
  - 'Window on the Universe (WOU)'.

Technical language

Obviously, the writer has used the 'jargon' connected to the subject, eg

- it does not instruct you to:
  'Put the disc in that slot in the front of your computer ...'
- it instructs you to:
  'Insert the Window on the Universe (WOU) CD-Rom in the relevant drive on your computer'.

Graphics

As this is a complicated set of instructions, the writer has included a graphic of what you should see on the screen.

Writing assignment

Using a computer in school or at home, write a set of detailed instructions for one of the following:

- how to get your computer to print
- how to get onto the Internet
- how to send an e-mail.

Imagine that the person reading these instructions has never used a computer before. They must:

- be in a clear, logical order
- explain any technical terms
- show, through graphics or detailed description, what the user should see on the screen.

Personal choice

Choose one of the following assignments:

1. Choose a favourite computer game and write a set of simple instructions so that a younger child could play the game.
2. Imagine you have followed the CD-Rom instructions but you have not been able to get into it. Write a letter to the manufacturer explaining exactly what the problem is.

Lake Kariba.

Although the building of the Kariba Dam was surrounded by controversy, both environmentally and socially, it is an impressive monument to man's engineering expertise. The massive valley, which now forms Lake Kariba has survived, with most plant and animal species having adapted to the changed conditions. Once Zambia realises the huge tourist potential the lake offers, there are many positive implications for the struggling economy and unemployment problems in the area. The Tonga People, whose traditional lands lie buried beneath the lake, would probably benefit most from tourist development.

When the dam was completed in 1960 it was the largest man-made dam ever built. Two hundred and twenty kilometres long and in places up to forty kilometres wide, it provides considerable electric power to both Zambia and Zimbabwe and supports a thriving commercial fishing industry. The lake's vastness creates spectacular panoramas as the sun casts its glow across the shimmering waters catching the distinctive half-submerged trees and islands.

History

The dam was an initiative of the Federation existing at the time between British ruled Northern and Southern Rhodesia (now Zambia and Zimbabwe) and Nyasaland (Malawi). To dam the great Zambezi floodplain was in many ways a hopeful leap into the future. Vast areas of forest and scrub would be inundated. Literally thousands of wild animals would lose their habitats and, more importantly, the local villages would have to be relocated. Analysis of the economic advantages convinced the authorities that the ultimate benefit to the people would outweigh the loss of wildlife and disturbance to people's lives.

The vegetation was strip cleared and burnt, making the lake rich in chemicals from the fired wood and the considerable number of remaining trees provided an essential habitat for many creatures that found their way into the lake.

Building the dam wall began in the late 1950s. Well over a million cubic metres of concrete was poured into the 36.6 metre high wall with a thickness of over twenty-four metres to sustain the pressure of nearly ten million litres of water passing through the spillway each second. At the end of 1958, the sluice gates were closed and in 1963 the maximum level was reached.

Nyaminyami

The name Kariba refers to a rock which thrust out of the swirling water at the entrance to the gorge close to the dam wall site, now buried more than a hundred feet below the water surface. In many legends, this rock was regarded as the home of the great River god Nyaminyami, who caused anyone who ventured near to be sucked down for ever into the depths of the river.

When the valley people heard they were to be moved from their tribal lands and the great Zambezi River blocked, they believed it would anger the river god so much that he would cause the water to boil and destroy the white man's bridge with floods.

In 1957, a year into the building of the dam, the river rose to flood level, pumping through the gorge with immense power, destroying some equipment and the access roads. The odds against another flood occurring the following year were about a thousand to one – but flood it did – three metres higher than the previous year. This time destroying the access bridge, the coffer dam and parts of the main wall. Nyaminyami had made good his threat. He had recaptured the gorge. His waters passed over the wreckage of his enemies at more than sixteen million litres a second, a flood which, it had been calculated, would only happen once in ten thousand years. Although man eventually won the battle when the dam was finally opened in 1960, there was a whole new respect for the power of the river god.

The displaced tribe

Within the area lived over fifty thousand people, mostly of the Batonga tribe, many of whom were vehemently against moving. Although land was set aside for them further up the valley, they were reluctant to leave their tribal lands and felt the move from the riverside would displease Nyaminyami. When the floods came and did in fact destroy parts of the bridge, this only served to confirm their fears. It took many months of reasoning and coaxing to convince the people that the bridge would provide power – a luxury they had no knowledge of – for the whole country. Eventually, however, when the trucks moved in to relocate them, they conceded, having little choice. Ceremonies were held to honour their gods and the journey to new lands began. Schools and clinics were built in some of the new areas and wells installed for their arrival. Some

new villages that were relocated close to the water's edge have prospered with the new fishing opportunities on the lake. But many mourn the loss of the rich alluvial river soil and battle to produce crops in the higher sandier areas. For the most part, the move was a severe disruption of their way of life and compensation minimal.

In recognition of this the Zambia Electricity Supply Company (Zesco) has established the Gwembe-Tonga project which aims to address some of the environmental and social issues which came about following the construction of the dam.

Road rehabilitation, the provision of a clean water supply, electrification, construction of schools, improving agricultural production, provision of technical assistance and health improvement are the core issues that the project will grapple with.

And in order to avoid some of the mistakes of the past the local communities are being involved in all stages of the project. The project implementation strategy will be based on a cost-sharing basis with the beneficiary and other resources while the community will be expected to provide manual labour and some raw materials.

Funding for the project which will cost about US$12,642,000, has been sourced from World Bank and Development Bank of Southern Africa (DBSA). The beneficiary community is expected to contribute 25% of the project cost. And government will contribute to the funding through the Rural Electrification Fund.

Operation Noah

As the dam began to fill, it became evident that thousands of animals were being stranded on islands. Appeals were made and money raised to buy boats and equipment for their rescue and relocation. This project became known as Operation Noah. It was a mammoth task and beset by numerous hazards. Submerged trees and stumps threatened the hulls of the boats and on the islands there were huge concentrations of snakes including the deadly black mamba. Even so, many were successfully rescued.

One story tells of a game ranger who climbed a tree in a swimming costume and gloves to catch a mamba with a noosed stick. Another tells of the rescue of a black rhino stranded on a small island. The animal was pursued for several hours until eventually it was driven past a marksman with a crossbow loaded with a muscle relaxing dart. Suitably sedated, the rhino was rolled on to a sledge, dragged ashore and loaded onto a raft buoyed up by eighteen petrol drums. Raft, rhino and all were then towed to the mainland some twelve miles away. An astonishing forty-four rhinos were rescued in this way. In all some 7000 animals were saved during Operation Noah. But there were many utterly tragic stories too. Scenes of stranded monkeys perching on treetops, unable to swim to shore, starving, every bit of greenery on the tree long eaten, their skins rotting in the water and too afraid of humans to allow themselves to be rescued. Countless smaller animals, reptiles and insects simply drowned. It was a reflection of the dominance of colonial rule in Salisbury, Southern Rhodesia, that most of the rescued animals were relocated to the Zimbabwean side and most of the people, to the Zambian side.

TEXT LEVEL WORK

Comprehension

A 1 Who originally lived on the land that is now submerged beneath Lake Kariba?

2 When was the dam completed?

3 What was the British name for:

a Zambia?
b Zimbabwe?
c Malawi?

4 According to legend, where did the river god Nyaminyami live?

5 Explain what Operation Noah was set up to do.

B 1 Explain the following in your own words:

a 'spectacular panoramas'
b 'essential habitat'
c 'confirm their fears'.

2 What advantages for the local people did those who supported the building of the dam put forward?

3 What disadvantages were there for the local people?

4 Explain in your own words what effect the building of the dam had on the local environment.

C Read through the explanation carefully and write chronological notes on how the dam was built.

WORD LEVEL WORK

Vocabulary

Dictionary and contextual work
Use a dictionary and the context of the passage to explain the meanings of the following words:

1 controversy	5 inundated	9 beneficiary
2 potential	6 vehemently	10 mammoth
3 thriving	7 conceded	11 buoyed
4 initiative	8 prospered	12 dominance

Spelling

'ance' words
Key words: disturb**ance**   entr**ance**   assist**ance**   domin**ance**

1 Use these key words in sentences of your own.

2 Learn these important 'ance' words:

perform**ance**   relev**ance**   irrelev**ance**   rom**ance**

bal**ance**   dist**ance**   assist**ance**

SENTENCE LEVEL WORK

Grammar and punctuation

Auxiliary verbs

> Remember. Most verbs are action words, but a few verbs indicate state of being or existence, eg
>
>> 'is', 'am', 'are', 'was', 'were', 'be', 'being', 'been', 'seem', 'look', 'feel', 'become'.
>
> These do not show actions, they just show that something exists. A verb can be more than one word – it is then called a *verb phrase*. Using auxiliary or 'helping' verbs makes verb phrases. An *auxiliary verb* works with the main verb to make tenses or moods. Auxiliary verbs include:
>
> - the modal verbs express the mood of verbs, eg
>
>> 'can', 'could', 'may', 'might', 'must', 'shall', 'should', 'will', 'would'
>
> - the primary verbs are able to work as main verbs or as auxiliary verbs, eg
>
>> 'be', 'do', 'have' and a few special verbs like 'dare' and 'need'
>
> - the verbs 'to be', 'to have' and 'to do'
> 'to be' is an auxiliary verb which shows continuing action, eg
>
>> *'I am going to the Kariba Dam.'*
>> *'We will be building the largest man-made dam.'*
>
> it also forms the passive voice, eg
>
>> *'Their food was fished from the lake.'*
>
> - 'to have' is an auxiliary verb for tenses that show completed action, eg
>
>> *'The tribe has resisted the move from the village in the past.'*
>> *'They hadn't wanted to move away.'*
>
> - 'to do' is an auxiliary verb for making questions and negatives, or to show emphasis, eg
>
>> *'Do you have any solutions to the problem?'*
>> *'He doesn't want Operation Noah to fail.'*
>> *'They do want the animals to be rescued.'*

Copy these sentences. Underline, colour or highlight the auxiliary verbs.

1 The game ranger is trying to catch the snake.
2 Do you have any opinions about the building of the dam?
3 The valley people hadn't wanted to anger the river god.
4 The government will be monitoring the progress of the project.
5 They did work hard to save the animals.
6 The animals and the people were relocated by the government.

TEXT LEVEL WORK

Writing

Explanatory writing

> Part of the article Lake Kariba is an *explanation*. It explains:
> - why the lake was made
> - how the lake was made
> - the effects on people and animals.

Language features

Introduction
The first paragraph of an explanation should give the reader a clear idea of what you are explaining. In the first paragraph we learn that the building of the Kariba dam:

'*was surrounded by controversy ...*'

'*... is an impressive monument to man's engineering expertise ...*'.

Organisation
After introducing what is to be explained, the paragraphs should take the reader through the explanation. In this article, the writer has used sub-headings to show which aspect of the topic he is writing about, eg

- History: how the dam was built
- Nyaminyami: details of an unusual flood
- The displaced tribe: the effect on the people and what was done
- Operation Noah: the effect on the animals and what was done.

Tense
Usually, an explanation is written in the present tense, eg

'*Once Zambia realises ...*'

'*The lake's vastness creates ...*'

'*The name Kariba refers to ...*'.

Parts of this article are written in the past tense because it is explaining something that has happened and is now completed, eg

'*The vegetation was stripped, cleared and burnt ...*'

'*Although land was set aside ...*'.

Writing assignment
Imagine you were involved in the rescue of the black rhino (Operation Noah). Write an explanatory report of how the rescue was accomplished. You will need to include:

- an introductory paragraph to make it clear what you are explaining
- following paragraphs explaining the steps of the rescue.

Personal choice

Choose one of the following assignments.

1 Imagine that the Kariba dam was not yet built but was being seriously considered. Either use the information in the article:

- to write a short report which supports the building of the dam
  or
- to write a short report which is against the building of the dam.

  Your report should explain the effects of building the dam on the people and animals.

2 Research Lake Kariba as a holiday destination. Write a paragraph to go in a tourist brochure, designed to persuade people to go there on holiday.

...the sunless depths.

Scientists Close in on Elusive Giant Squid

The lair of the giant squid is a staple of novels and horror movies, and perhaps of nightmares. But for biologists it is a mystery. No one has ever observed the beast in its natural habitat, despite decades of probing the sea's dim recesses. Fishermen towing nets through the depths have snagged giant squids on occasion, and dead or dying ones have been known to wash ashore, often half eaten by birds and sea life. But more than a century after the giant squid and its supposed habitat were featured in "20,000 Leagues Under the Sea," the surprising truth is that very little is known of the deep monster and how it eats and rests, courts and mates, swims and behaves.

That may soon change, however. Scientists have made much progress lately in discovering the giant's den. In the last two months alone, biologists and fishermen around New Zealand and Australia have cast nets into the deep and caught four of the big squids, including one of the largest males ever found. Moreover, a leading expert on the creatures, Dr. Clyde F. E. Roper of the National Museum of Natural History at the Smithsonian Institution in Washington, is mounting a $5 million expedition to observe the giant squid in its habitat. Travelling to the South Pacific near New Zealand, Roper plans to enter a tiny submersible, dive deep and shadow the beast in the sunless depths, seeking to capture its secrets on film for the first time. "Our chances are very, very good," Roper said of the possibility of a deep encounter. "But keep in mind that we had lots of shots at the Moon before we got there." Referring to the cost of the New Zealand foray, he added: "It's a relatively tiny investment when you think of the potential for knowledge and information. We know so little about their biology and behaviour." Roper has studied the giant squid for decades but, like all other experts, has never seen one alive. Specimens hauled to the surface are usually dead or about to expire, having been battered, squeezed and suffocated in nets full of fish.

The main clues that Roper and other scientists have followed to locate the animal's habitat are food chains – the progression of who eats whom in nature, from microscopic grazers to mammoth predators the size of apartment buildings. It turns out that the giant squid feeds on certain types of deep fish now being harvested in great numbers and in turn is fed on by sperm whales, giants in their own right that dive down perhaps up to a mile to feast on the boneless leviathans. Scientists, like hunters following a pack of bloodhounds, plan on tracking the fauna at both ends of this food chain in hopes of discovering the giant squid in the middle, lurking in its dark home. Some experts are a bit leery about doing so, given the beast's 10 large tentacles lined with sucker pads and its reputation for ruthlessness. "I have a lot of respect for these animals," said Dr. Ellen C. Forch, a fisheries biologist in New Zealand, who for more than 15 years has compiled data on the giant squid. As for the expedition, Dr. Forch said she had no plans to go down in the tiny submersible and preferred to monitor the action from a ship. "I have two small children," she explained. "And they need their mother."

Though very poorly known, and often used as a symbol of humanity's ignorance of the deep, the giant squid already holds a number of records. It is believed to be the largest of all the world's creatures that have no backbones, growing up to lengths of 60 or 70 feet, longer than a city bus. Its huge eyes are the largest in the animal kingdom, sometimes the size of dinner plates. Some of its nerve fibres are so big they were initially mistaken for blood vessels.

Over the centuries the giant squid has clearly been the inspiration for countless tales of ogres, including the kraken, legendary sea monsters off Norway. Erik Pontoppidan, bishop of Bergen, a Norwegian port, in 1753 described an immense sea monster 'full of arms' that was big enough to crush the largest man-of-war. Modern impressions of the giant squid began to form with Jules Verne's '20,000 Leagues Under the Sea,' which was published in Paris in 1871. Drawing on reports of real-life encounters, he depicted the animal fairly accurately anatomically but fabricated its habitat, describing it as living in deep caverns in the sides of submarine cliffs. The cave openings were cloaked by tangles of giant weeds. As Captain Nemo and his submarine passed one of these dim grottoes, a passenger saw a 'formidable swarming, wriggling movement' in the weeds. Soon, the submarine and its crew were battling a swarm of giant squids and their writhing tentacles. In the 20th century, it became clear from sightings, captures and strandings that the giant squid was ubiquitous throughout the sea, though very reclusive. Its scientific name is Architeuthis (pronounced ark-e-TOOTH-iss), meaning chief squid in Greek ...

The scientific team consisting of the New Zealanders, Dr. Roper and his Smithsonian colleagues believe that the time is ripe to make a concerted push to observe the giant squid in its habitat. "Seeing a giant squid would be the ultimate," said Dr. Forch, the fisheries biologist. "Naturalists for a long time have been going after all sorts of exotic things that are easy to get to. But this is very remote and elusive. It's just out of reach."

If enough money can be raised, the team plans to conduct the hunt between late November and February, which is summertime in New Zealand and a season when the giants are frequently found. In a two-pronged attack, the team first plans to use the research vessel Tangaroa to make preliminary searches for deep fish types and densities. Then, its specialists will deploy binoculars up top and underwater microphones below to track and listen to sperm whales as they dive into the depths to eat squid, hopefully guiding the scientists to the lair.

If all goes as planned, team members plan to send a robot down to inspect the area and then to dive personally into the inky darkness in the Johnson Sea-Link, a submersible operated by the Harbor Branch Oceanographic Institution in Fort Pierce, Fla. Outfitted with robotic arms, lights and video cameras, the submersible is made of a single large acrylic sphere for maximum visibility and can carry up to four people to depths of 3,000 feet, well within the bounds of the beast's apparent home. Teaming up with the scientists will be National Geographic, which plans to televise the encounter.

"If we find one and film it, that would be absolutely spectacular," said Roper, who seems to have no fear that the submersible will be wrapped in giant tentacles and crushed or crippled. "A few minutes of film would show a lot," he said. "Seeing a giant squid from a submersible would open a new world of understanding."

William J Broad

TEXT LEVEL WORK

Comprehension

A 1 Although scientists have found '*dead or dying*' giant squids, what have they never been able to do?

2 How much is the expedition which is being mounted by Dr Roper going to cost?

3 How have Dr Roper and other scientists been able to locate where giant squids live?

4 To what length can a giant squid grow?

5 When do the team plan to '*conduct the hunt*'?

B 1 Explain the following in your own words:

   a '*a bit leery*'
   b '*fabricated its habitat*'
   c '*was ubiquitous*'.

2 The scientists on the project are described as '*hunters following a pack of bloodhounds*'. What impression does this give you of the scientists?

3 When Dr Roper is quoted as saying, '*But keep in mind that we had lots of shots at the Moon before we got there*', what is he trying to convey about the expedition?

4 What impression do you get of:

   • Dr Roper?
   • Dr Forch?

C Find one example of each of the following in the report:

   • a fact   • an opinion   • a statistic.

WORD LEVEL WORK

Vocabulary

Dictionary and contextual work

Use a dictionary and the context of the passage to explain the meanings of the following words:

1 lair	5 potential	9 anatomically
2 recesses	6 leviathans	10 fabricated
3 expedition	7 leery	11 ubiquitous
4 encounter	8 inspiration	12 reclusive

Spelling

'sion' words

Key words: occa**sion**   progre**ssion**   impre**ssion**

1 Use these key words in sentences of your own.

2 Learn these important 'sion' words:

   conclu**sion**   deci**sion**   persua**sion**   posse**ssion**

   dimen**sion**   illu**sion**   ten**sion**

SENTENCE LEVEL WORK

Grammar and punctuation

Irregular verbs

Remember. All verbs have five forms known as *principal parts*, whether they are regular or irregular. These forms are:
1 the infinitive, eg 'to do'
2 simple present, eg 'I do'
3 simple past, eg 'I did'
4 past participle, eg 'have done'
5 present participle, eg 'doing'.

Regular verbs are consistent – the past tense ends in 'ed' and so does the past participle.

Infinitive	to observe	to probe	to wash
Simple present	observe(s)	probe(s)	wash(es)
Simple past	observed	probed	washed
Past participle	observed	probed	washed
Present participle	observing	probing	washing

Irregular verbs end in different ways, with no regular pattern.

Infinitive	to arise	to begin	to catch
Simple present	arise(s)	begin(s)	catch(es)
Simple past	arose	began	caught
Past participle	arisen	begun	caught
Present participle	arising	beginning	catching

Copy and complete this table.

Infinitive	Simple present	Simple past	Past participle	Present participle
to be				
to eat				
to lie (to rest or recline)				
to sit				
to write				

TEXT LEVEL WORK

Writing

Newspaper article

Scientists Close in on Elusive Giant Squid appeared in the science section of *The New York Times*. Because of the specialist nature of the content and because it is not a 'report' about one particular current event, writings of this kind which appear in newspapers are called 'articles' rather than reports. It is not about something that has happened, but rather about something that is being planned.

Language features

Headline

Headlines are designed to grab the reader's attention. The headline is deliberately misleading to give the impression that scientists have accomplished more than they actually have! What difference in effect would this headline have?

> **Scientists think they might be able to photograph a giant squid**

Introduction

The introduction must work like the headline and draw the reader in. To appeal to a wider audience than just those with a scientific background, the writer has begun by explaining the mystery of the giant squid:

> *'The lair of the giant squid is a staple of novels and horror movies ...'.*

Beginning with a list of facts and figures about the squid would put some people off.

Interesting vocabulary

To continue the 'air of mystery' the writer has chosen interesting, vivid language, eg

> *'... the giant's den ...'*; *'... shadow the beast in the sunless depths ...'.*

Factual information

The factual information about the giant squid is 'spread out' throughout the article so that the reader is not 'put off' by endless statistics, eg

- Paragraph 3: facts relating to the food chain
- Paragraph 4: facts about the giant squid's size and anatomy.

Future tense

The article is partly about what the scientists plan to do to learn more, so the writer uses the future tense, eg

> *'... its specialists will deploy binoculars ...'*
> *'Teaming up with scientists will be the National Geographic ...'.*

Expert opinion

The experts are the people who are actually taking part in the expedition. The writer gives their qualifications so the reader feels that they know what they are talking about, eg

> *'... a leading expert on the creatures, Dr. Clyde F. E. Roper of the National Museum of Natural History at the Smithsonian Institution in Washington ...'.*

The writer has obviously interviewed these people to gain first hand information, eg

> Dr Forch: *'I have a lot of respect for these animals ...'.*

Writing assignment

Research either the Loch Ness Monster or the Yeti and write a newspaper article about a fictitious expedition which is being prepared to find the creature. You should include:

- an attention grabbing headline
- what is known about the creature to date
- how the scientists hope to track down the creature
- expert opinion.

Personal choice

Choose one of the following assignments.

1 Imagine you are one of the scientists who goes down in the 'tiny submersible' and comes face-to-face with a giant squid. Write a factual report of the surroundings, the giant squid's lair and the squid itself.

2 The expedition in the article needs funds – *'If enough money can be raised'*. Write a letter to a large company asking for a contribution to the $5 million which you need. You should explain:

- what is involved in the expedition
- why it is so important.

Black Sea Artifacts may be Evidence of Biblical Flood

By Guy Gugliotta
Washington Post Staff Writer
Wednesday, September 13, 2000

Archaeologists said yesterday they have discovered the remains of a man-made structure more than 300 feet below the surface of the Black Sea, providing dramatic new evidence of an apocalyptic flood 7,500 years ago that may have inspired the Biblical story of Noah.

The expedition also spotted planks, beams, tree branches and chunks of wood untouched by worms or mollusks, a strong indication that the oxygen-free waters of the Black Sea's 7,000-foot-deep abyss may shelter intact shipwrecks dating back to the dawn of seafaring.

"It is beyond our wildest imagination," explorer Robert D. Ballard, leader of the expedition, said yesterday. "Wood is existing much shallower than we thought. When we do go deep, it can only get better."

The discovery is the latest from the Black Sea project to look for ancient shipwrecks and perhaps evidence of a great flood. Late last year, the team discovered the outlines of an ancient coast 550 feet below the current waterline, the first visual evidence that a flood had occurred in the region eons ago.

This month, working from a ship 12 miles east of the Turkish port city of Synope, Ballard's team used special 'side-scan' sonar to map anomalies on the sea floor, then sent a robotic submersible to investigate the most promising sites.

At 311 feet, the submersible found a collapsed rectangular building 39 feet long and 13 feet wide, "about like a good-sized barn," Ballard said in a telephone interview from the site.

University of Pennsylvania archaeologist Fredrik Hiebert described the construction technique as a 'cluster of wood stuck in a clay matrix' – traditional Black Sea 'wattle and daub' architecture: "This struck a bell, because it was familiar to me from land," Hiebert said. "Literally my jaw dropped."

The expedition also found old tree branches, pieces of wood and a trash heap with polished stones and other debris indicating human habitation, Ballard said.

In the same general area, the submersible identified two old shipwrecks with many intact wooden planks and ceramic amphorae – jars used in ancient times to transport liquids such as olive oil or wine. Researchers are unsure if they are from the same period or related to an ancient flooded settlement.

Archaeologists have long been interested in the Black Sea, because its waters are anoxic – lacking in oxygen – below a depth of 500 feet. In theory, organic material that shipworms quickly gobble elsewhere would lie untouched in the Black Sea's sterile depths. Later this month Ballard plans the first-ever exploration of the Black Sea floor.

Interest in the Black Sea quickened last year with the publication of 'Noah's Flood,' by Columbia University geologists William Ryan and Walter Pitman, suggesting that the modern-day sea was formed 7,500 years ago when melting glaciers raised sea levels until the waters of the Mediterranean breached

the natural dam at the Bosphorus.

According to the theory, a cataclysmic deluge followed. Seawater from the Mediterranean poured into the Black Sea basin at 200 times the volume of Niagara Falls. The heavier salt water plunged to the bottom of the existing fresh water lake and began to fill the basin like a bathtub.

The theory holds that the rising lake-sea inundated and submerged thousands of square miles of land, destroying communities, killing people and wiping out uncounted species of plants and animals as the ecosystem flipped from fresh water to salt water in a period of only two years.

The flood also created a two-layered body of water, which permanently interfered with the normal convection that brings deep water to the surface for oxygenation. The less dense fresh water lay like a lid on top of the denser Mediterranean water, sterile once its original oxygen had been used up. Today the top 500 feet of the Black Sea supports a thriving marine life, but the rest is as dead as the ancient day when the flood waters settled.

Scholars regard both the book of Genesis and the story of Noah as legends written between 2,900 and 2,500 years ago, and have questioned whether any natural disaster could be conclusively identified as the inspiration for Noah's flood.

Still, the event described by Ryan and Pitman appears horrible enough to be remembered by scribes and poets long enough to become the source of the Biblical story.

"Among scholars who take the Bible literally this will be confirmation," said Hershel Shanks, editor of Biblical Archaeology Review. "Critical Bible scholars are almost unanimous in regarding the flood story as a legend. On the other hand, legends arise not out of imagination but from an experience. I don't think we'll ever know what flood that was."

Last year, Ballard's expedition, which is supported by the National Geographic Society, the Office of Naval Research, the National Oceanic and Atmospheric Administration, the J.M. Kaplan Fund and the University of Pennsylvania, discovered evidence of an old coast.

Tests of shell samples showed that freshwater mollusks had lived in the waters until 7,500 years ago, but had been replaced with marine species 600 years later. The next question, Ballard said, was "did anyone live here?"

On land, Hiebert's archaeological work at Synope suggested that the likeliest spot for settlements was between 165 feet and 330 feet above sea level. The 'sweet spot' for pre-flood communities, therefore, should be in waters 170 feet to 435 feet deep, he said.

On Sept. 2, Ballard's team began to scan this band of territory: "if you drained it back, it would be rolling countryside with meandering streams," Ballard said. "We located the countryside, and located the river systems."

Shortly after that, they found the submerged building with intact wood about 200 feet above where they expected to find it: "Now we're looking for the neighbours," Ballard said.

TEXT LEVEL WORK

Comprehension

A 1 How long ago was the 'apocalyptic flood' thought to have taken place?

2 What did the submersible find at 311 feet?

3 Why can the scientists find intact wooden objects in the 'anoxic' waters of the Black Sea?

4 Why does marine life only exist in the top 500 feet of water of the Black Sea?

5 What organisations are supporting Ballard's expedition?

B 1 Explain the following in your own words:

a 'a strong indication'
b 'beyond our wildest imagination'
c 'This struck a bell'.

2 What does the fact that Hiebert's 'jaw dropped' tell you about his reaction to the construction of the building the submersible found?

3 What do you understand is the attitude of:

a 'those people who take the bible literally'?
b 'Critical Bible scholars'?

4 What conclusions have scientists come to after discovering submerged buildings?

C Using the information in the passage, copy and complete the table to show how Ryan and Pitman suggest the Black Sea was formed.

Stage 1:	Melting glaciers raised the sea level
Stage 2:	
Stage 3:	A huge flood occurred
Stage 4:	
Stage 5:	The rising lake-sea swept over the surrounding land
Stage 6:	

WORD LEVEL WORK

Vocabulary

Dictionary and contextual work

Use a dictionary and the context of the passage to explain the meanings of the following words:

1 apocalyptic	4 anomalies	7 breached	10 convection
2 visual	5 debris	8 cataclysmic	11 unanimous
3 eons	6 sterile	9 ecosystem	12 meandering

Spelling

'al' words

Key words: tradition**al**   origin**al**   natur**al**

1 Use these key words in sentences of your own.

2 Learn these important 'al' words:

miner**al**   physic**al**   region**al**   chemic**al**   biblic**al**   buri**al**   rur**al**

SENTENCE LEVEL WORK

Grammar and punctuation

Adverbs

> Remember. *Adverbs* tell us how, when or where the action of the verb takes place. Many adverbs are formed by adding 'ly' to an adjective, eg
>
> quick + ly = quickly.
>
> Adjectives give us further detail/information about nouns, eg
>
> *Biblical* flood.

Copy and complete the table. Tick the correct column to show whether each word in bold is an adjective or an adverb.

Sentence	Adjective	Adverb
providing **dramatic** new evidence		
shelter **intact** shipwrecks		
beyond our **wildest** imagination		
permanently interfered with the normal convection		
ancient shipwrecks		
evidence of an **apocalyptic** flood		
robotic submersible to investigate		
conclusively identified as the inspiration		
collapsed rectangular building		
traditional Black Sea 'wattle and daub'		
Literally my jaw dropped		
thriving **marine** life		

TEXT LEVEL WORK

Writing

Feature article

> Articles such as *Black Sea Artifacts may be Evidence of Biblical Flood* use many different styles of writing and, as such, do different 'jobs'.

Language features

Information

Parts of the article are informative. A reader needs to know factual information about the subject, eg

'... *the Black Sea's 7,000-foot-deep abyss* ...'

'... *its waters are anoxic – lacking in oxygen – below a depth of 500 feet* ...'.

Explanation

Other parts of the article are designed to explain processes which will help the reader to understand how and why things might have occurred, eg

'... *created a two-layered body of water, which permanently interfered with the normal convection that brings deep water to the surface for oxygenation.*'

Opinion

The writer offers opinions as well as facts, eg

'*Researchers are unsure if they are from the same period ...*'
'*According to the theory, a cataclysmic deluge followed ...*'.

Interview style

The writer has interviewed people involved in the project to get first hand comments, eg

'... *"about like a good size barn," Ballard said in a telephone interview from the site.*'
'*Hiebert said, "Literally, my jaw dropped."*'

Writing assignment

Research one of the following:

- the sinking of the *Titanic*
- the raising of the *Mary Rose*.

Write a feature article which includes:

- information
- explanation
- opinions
- first hand comments.

Personal choice

Choose one of the following assignments.

1 Research the Black Sea and present the information in the form of a fact file.
2 'Archaeology is a waste of money.' Do you agree or disagree with this statement? Explain your reasons.

. . . seeing fairies . . .

The Legend:

In July 1917, 16-year-old Elsie Wright and her 10-year-old cousin Frances Griffiths were tired of being chided by Elsie's father over their claims of seeing fairies ... so they took a photograph of some to prove their existence.

The girls lived together in Cottingley, on the outskirts of Bradford, West Yorkshire, England. They often played together in the small wooded creek behind Elsie's home, and this is where they saw the fairies. On a day in July, Elsie, tired of her father's dismissive attitude to her and Frances' claims, borrowed her father's camera to take a picture. When the film was developed later in her father's dark room, Elsie's parents were in for a surprise; the picture that she had taken was of Frances ... with a troop of fairies dancing in front of her.

Elsie's parents were flabbergasted; but her father wasn't convinced. So, a month later, Frances took a picture of Elsie which clearly showed her playing with a gnome. Mr. Wright still wasn't convinced, and there the matter settled. The girls showed the pictures to their friends, but no particular interest was ever raised by them ... at least, not until two years had passed.

Elsie's mother had developed an interest in things supernatural, and took the pictures to share with a Theosophist meeting in Bradford one evening. In no time at all, the pictures were the centre of attention and argument. Of the people who believed the fairies were real, the most prominent and vocal was Sir Arthur Conan Doyle, creator of Sherlock Holmes. Sir Arthur printed the first two pictures in *Strand Magazine* in 1920 to help support his argument for the existence of fairies; this article made the story a worldwide sensation.

In 1920, Sir Arthur arranged for Elsie and Frances to once again be given a camera and left on their own in the small creek. The results were three more photos of the fairies; the last to be made, for shortly after Elsie and Frances moved away from one another and stopped seeing fairies. Sir Arthur later printed these three pictures in a sequel to his earlier article, and, in 1922, he expanded the two articles into a book, *The Coming of the Fairies*.

The Rest of the Story ...

While the legend of the Cottingley Fairies as told in a number of popular magazines and children's books over the years may end as the account above does, there is some more to be added to the situation now.

The controversy over the pictures continued to rage into the 1960s, when new techniques for examining the photos brought them more into question. Elsie's position on the matter became vague. In 1966 she was quoted as saying she had photographed 'figments of my imagination,' and in 1971 on BBC TV in England she said that she just wanted to leave the subject 'open.' [Quotes are according to Jenny Randles in *Strange & Unexplained Mysteries of the 20th Century*.] In 1976 during a YTV 'Calendar' interview, Frances (now 69) and Elsie (now 75) were asked, "Did you in any way fabricate those photographs?" Elsie answered firmly: "Of course not." Frances' answer was interesting: "You tell us how she could do it ... and then we'll tell you. ... Remember, she was sixteen. And I was ten."

In 1982, Geoffrey Crawley, then the editor of the British Journal of Photography, published an article detailing his examination of what was believed to be the original negatives of the Cottingley photographs in the Brotherton Collection of Leeds University. His argument was simple; the 'Midg' style camera that was used by the girls to take the first two photographs was, by design, incapable of producing negatives as clearly defined as the negatives that were in the Brotherton Collection. Amazingly, he managed to find what appears to be an original print of the first photo in Cottingley; a comparison of this original to a print made from the Brotherton negatives is startling.

The original is muddy and fuzzy; Frances' face can just be made out, and the 'fairies' are just splotches of white – and, as Crawley says in *Arthur C. Clarke's World of Strange Powers*, "... exactly the type of, shall we say, less lively image that you would expect from a camera of this type." A closer examination of the negatives in the Brotherton Collection revealed evidence of airbrush retouching to make the fairies more defined, and of burnishing to help drop Frances' face into the background. The popular version of the photos that was being presented in the press and books were fraudulent.

In an article in the *Times* of London for March 18, 1983, 76-year-old Frances Griffiths admitted the first four pictures were faked; now 82-year-old Elsie Wright Hill at first refused to comment, but in a second article on April 4 she confirmed the hoax. They had cut out figures drawn on bristol board by Elsie, and stood them up with hat-pins. The fairies in the first photo were traced from an illustration of dancing girls that came from page 104 of a copy of 'Princess Mary's Gift Book.'

But the two disagreed on the fifth picture; mainly each woman claimed to have been the one to take it. Frances stated that it was the only genuine photo, and Elsie claimed "it was all done with my own contraption and I had to wait for the weather to be right to take it."

This last seeming controversy was quickly given a logical explanation by none other than Geoffrey Crawley. In a letter to the *Times* on April 9, 1983, Crawley pointed out the fifth and last photo, called 'Fairies and Their Sun-Bath' by Sir Arthur, was previously studied in 1972 by Brian Coe, Curator of the Kodak Museum. Coe concluded it was a double exposure of fairy cutouts in grass, which explains why both women were convinced they had taken the photo ... both had.

© 2002 Garth Haslam

TEXT LEVEL WORK

Comprehension

A 1 How old were Elsie Wright and Frances Griffiths, in 1917?

2 Where did the girls live?

3 At which meeting, in Bradford, did Elsie's mother show the photographs?

4 Which famous author publicised the photographs?

5 Which book did the girls use for their illustrations?

B 1 Why did the girls decide to carry out the hoax?

2 In which book did a famous author expand his earlier articles about the 'Cottingley Fairies'?

3 Why did Geoffrey Crawley claim that the '*popular version of the photos that was being presented in the press and books were fraudulent*'?

4 When, and in which articles, did the girls finally admit that they had carried out a hoax?

C 1 Why do you think that the girls differed in their later explanations about the photographs? You should consider disagreements about:

   a whether the photographs were genuine or fake
   b who took which photographs.

2 Why do you think that some adults were prepared to believe the girls' story, while others were not? Quote from the passage in support of your answer.

WORD LEVEL WORK

Vocabulary

Dictionary and contextual work

Use a dictionary and the context of the passage to explain the meanings of the following words:

1	chided	5	supernatural	9	figments
2	dismissive	6	prominent	10	splotches
3	flabbergasted	7	sequel	11	contraption
4	gnome	8	controversy	12	hoax

Spelling

'ence' words

Key words: exist**ence**   evid**ence**

1 Use these key words in sentences of your own.

2 Learn these important 'ence' words:

   consci**ence**   consequ**ence**   refer**ence**   sequ**ence**

   def**ence**   depend**ence**   prefer**ence**

SENTENCE LEVEL WORK

Grammar and punctuation

Simple and compound sentences

Remember. A *simple sentence* is made up of one main clause, which makes sense by itself, eg

   '*The girls lived in Cottingley.*'

A *compound sentence* is made up of two or more simple sentences joined by a conjunction, eg

   '*Mr. Wright still wasn't convinced, (and) there the matter settled.*'

     clause   conjunction   clause

Join each pair of simple sentences to make a compound sentence. Write down each compound sentence, underlining your two main clauses and putting a ring around the conjunction.

1 The girls showed the pictures to their friends.
   No particular interest was ever raised by them.

2 Elsie Wright Hill at first refused to comment.
   In a second article on April 4 she confirmed the hoax.

3 The girls were tired of being teased.
   They photographed the fairies.

4 They often played together.
   This is when they saw the fairies.

5 Elsie's parents were flabbergasted.
   Her father wasn't convinced.

TEXT LEVEL WORK

Writing

Research – presenting evidence

When writers try to present non-fiction information about an issue or situation, they will usually refer to a range of evidence from their research. The evidence is used to convince the reader that the writer knows what he/she is talking about. It is also used to give authority to what the writer is saying.

The evidence used by a writer is often the result of many hours of research, using a variety of techniques. The writer may use traditional paper sources, such as books, magazines and newspapers. However, increasingly, writers use electronic means, such as CD-ROMs and the Internet, with its sophisticated search engines. In addition, writers may interview experts or witnesses, to give their writing 'the ring of truth'.

Language features

References to data

When a writer seeks to inform readers, they will often make references to factual research information. This helps to give the writing a feeling of being real and may include:

- dates and times, eg *'In July 1917 ...'*
- places, eg *'The girls lived together in Cottingley, on the outskirts of Bradford, West Yorkshire, England.'*

Well-known authority figures

To lend authority to what they may be saying, writers find well-known people to back up their view. In the passage, the writer found evidence that suited this purpose, eg

'Sir Arthur Conan Doyle, creator of Sherlock Holmes ...'.

Sir Arthur Conan Doyle was a well-known, popular and influential writer of the time. He publicised the case, which not only gives authority to the writer's information but also actively promoted the events, eg

'Sir Arthur printed the first two pictures in Strand Magazine'.

'Expert' opinion

In addition to well-known figures such as Sir Arthur Conan Doyle, writers will try to find evidence of 'experts'. These 'experts', who are acknowledged to know a great deal about the subject, give credibility to the information being put forward by the writer, eg

'Geoffrey Crawley, then the editor of the British Journal of Photography ...'

As a prominent figure in the field of photography, his 'expert' opinion is both believable and convincing, eg

'... the 'Midg' style camera that was used by the girls to take the first two photographs was, by design, incapable of producing negatives as clearly defined as the negatives that were in the Brotherton Collection.'

Quotations from people 'who were there'

Another form of research used by writers to provide convincing information, is to find witnesses to interview. In the passage, the writer has researched the subject thoroughly and found evidence of a television interview with one of the girls responsible for the photographs, eg

'... in 1971 on BBC TV in England she said that she just wanted to leave the subject 'open'.'

Formal, sophisticated language

The passage is written in the third person, past tense, which is common in non-fiction writing to inform. In addition, in order to sound authoritative, the writer uses:

1 sophisticated vocabulary, eg *'flabbergasted'*; *'Theosophist'*

2 technical language, eg *'airbrush retouching'*; *'burnishing'*

3 complex sentence constructions, eg *'In a letter to the Times on April 9, 1983, Crawley pointed out the fifth and last photo, called 'Fairies and Their Sun-Bath' by Sir Arthur, was previously studied in 1972 by Brian Coe, Curator of the Kodak Museum.'*

This makes the author sound clever and knowledgeable, giving his writing an impression of being convincing.

Writing assignment

Research and make notes on one well-known 'hoax', eg

- UFOs
- ghosts and hauntings
- mysterious events.

Write a convincing passage of non-fiction writing to inform, on the 'hoax' of your choice. Remember to include as many of the following as you can:

- references to data
- well-known authority figures
- expert opinion
- quotations from people who were there
- formal, sophisticated language.

Personal choice

The 'Cottingley girls' took convincing photographs, as evidence for the existence of fairies. Choose one of the following assignments.

1 Write an explanation, and give examples, of the different types of evidence that researchers have used in their investigations of:

a the Bermuda Triangle

b the *Marie Celeste*

c crop circles.

2 Write a summary of the reasons why, and why not, the evidence is convincing, in one of the examples given above.

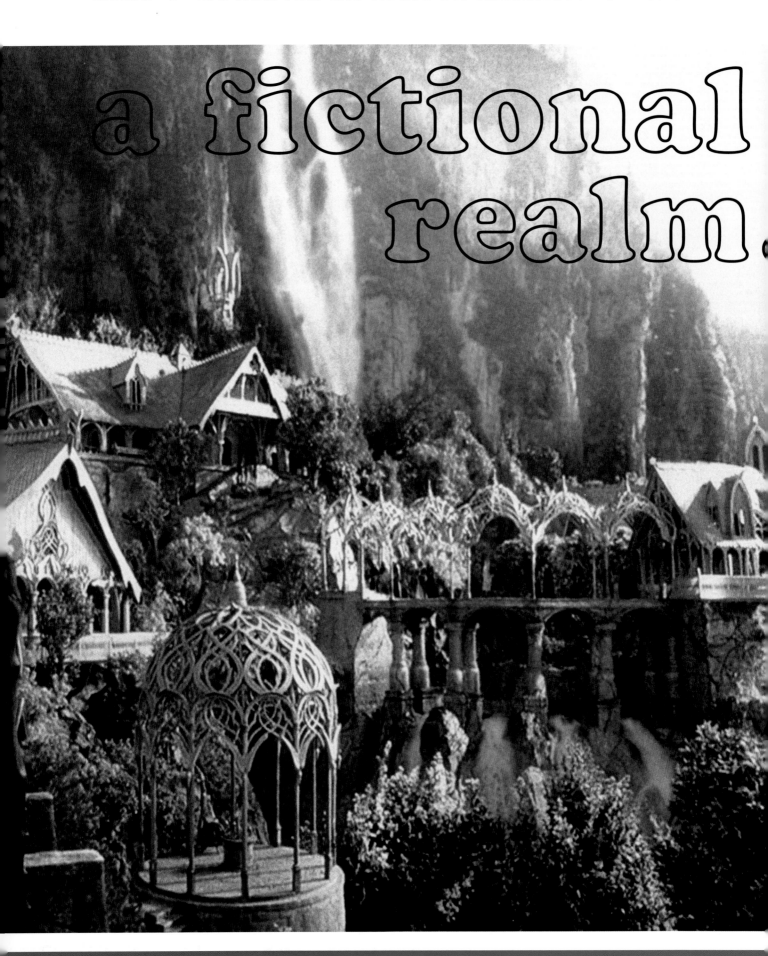

a fictional realm.

his is a curious door: green and round, with a shiny yellow brass knob in the middle. I would recognise it anywhere, but never supposed that I would find myself standing on the doorstep. Yet, after travelling halfway round the world to Wellington, New Zealand, here I am outside Bag End, in Hobbiton. It seems inconceivable that Bilbo Baggins and his cousin Frodo won't be inside, taking tea or sharing a pipe of one of their favourite tobaccos – Longbottom Leaf, perhaps, or Old Toby. Instead, when I push open the door, there is a blaze of fluorescent lights, the sound of drills and hammers, as set-builders and decorators fix fixtures, lay tiles, paint walls and varnish wooden beams ready for the arrival of the actors Ian Holm, Elijah Wood and Sir Ian McKellern. This is just a small corner of J R R Tolkien's fictional realm as seen through the eyes of the director Peter Jackson, and its authenticity is astonishing: the elaborately carved decoration of bulrushes around the fireplace, the leaded-glass windows, and the ornate wrought-iron hinge that swirls across the back of the front door like the tendrils of a fern. It is through this very door that Bilbo and, later, Frodo set out on their life-changing journeys. Whereas Bilbo's journey in The Hobbit was a Boy's Own Adventure-style jaunt in search of stolen dragon-gold, the sequel, The Lord of the Rings, was to take Frodo on a desperate quest: not to gain a great treasure, but to throw one away; against unthinkable odds, to attempt the destruction of a source of terrifying and all-corrupting power.

Inside Bag End is the New Zealand-born Peter Jackson, dressed in shorts and a T-shirt, as barefoot as a Hobbit. "Let's talk as we go," he says, so we head off for a five-minute drive along the road to the building where the digital animation unit works.

For Jackson, it all began with another journey: a 12-hour train ride from Wellington to Auckland when he was a teenager. He decided to take a book along to pass the time and, at a thousand pages long, The Lord of the Rings was the perfect volume. After reading just a few chapters, the young Jackson was lost among the wonders and terrors of Middle-earth. "As I read," he recalls, "my first thought was, 'I hope somebody will make a movie of this book, because I'd really like to see it.' Well, I waited 20 years and, as nobody else made it, I ended up making it myself." It sounds so simple. Almost as if filming three pictures concurrently wasn't an unprecedented venture in cinema history; as if the project hadn't been in the planning stage for nearly five years; and as if he hadn't been filming with scarcely a break now, for 14 months.

"There have been weeks," he admits, "when I've been simultaneously juggling all three movies: filming scenes with Frodo and Gandalf at Bag End for the Fellowship of the Ring; approving a costume design for King Theoden, whom you won't see until the second film; or looking at scale layouts of the set for the Grey Havens in the third movie." We've arrived at the animation studio, and immediately Jackson is on the run, pounding up and down staircases and along labyrinthine corridors. Today he is viewing a sequence in which the fellowship, struggling through the Orc-infested Mines of Moria, encounter a rampaging cave troll. A few seconds' worth of images are run over and over again on the computer screens while the animators describe what they are trying to achieve: the way in which a dim light is filtering down into the shadowy Dwarf mines and illuminating the troll's bulk; the way the brutish monster reacts when hit by a spear. Jackson studies this sequence and then acts out the move for the animator: "He's really not very bright, you see, so he's surprised."

Hunching his shoulders, the director is miming how the troll should pluck out the spear and look at it quizzically as if it were a toothpick. "He's hurt, but his reaction must also show his confusion." He repeats the pantomime, imitated by the animator. "Yeah, yeah!" he enthuses. "That's it!"

On we go, this time to view progress on a scene in the second film, where an army of Orcs besieges the ancient stronghold of Helm's Deep. "When we've finished this shot," says Jackson, "that empty plain is going to be seething with a vast army of Uruk-hai warriors – 10,000 digitally created Orcs with swords and spears and banners. Tolkien's writing is so vivid that you instantly 'see' the fantastical creatures and extraordinary places he is describing." It is one of those extraordinary places – the Elven haven of Lothlorien – that is my next destination. My guide is Jackson's longtime friend and associate Richard Taylor, the man behind Weta Workshop. This multiskilled unit is responsible for the special effects, and takes its name from the weta, a large New Zealand insect, not unlike a cockroach. Tall and bespectacled, Taylor bubbles with enthusiasm: "For us at Weta, The Lord of the Rings has been a journey of discovery: facing up to the amazing range of tasks that needed to be done, adapting skills we already possessed and then – day by day, step by step – learning and mastering new disciplines." As well as kitting out the equivalent of several large armies (900 suits of armour and 2,000 weapons), Weta has designed prosthetics such as Elf ears, wizard noses and 1,600 pairs of hairy Hobbit feet. "We've had an armourer working at an open forge crafting swords in the same way as they did in the Middle Ages," says Taylor. "We've made everything from hand-tooled leather armour fit for a king, through to thousands of grotesque body suits for the marauding hordes of Orcs – and, of course, all the miniature models for the film, such as Lothlorien."

Brian Sibley, The Sunday Times Magazine, 25 November 2001

TEXT LEVEL WORK

Comprehension

A 1 What is a 'weta'?

2 What is the name of the house, to which the door belongs?

3 What is the name of the director of *The Lord of the Rings*?

4 What are the names of Bilbo's and Frodo's favourite tobaccos?

5 What is the name of the elven haven?

B 1 Where does the fellowship encounter the cave troll?

2 What was the director trying to show the animator when he mimed the cave troll's actions?

3 What were the challenges faced by Weta Workshop?

4 How does the writer of the article, Brian Sibley, describe the differences between *The Hobbit* and *The Lord of the Rings*?

C 1 The writer of the article quotes statistics to make his account seem more precise, truthful and impressive. Find and copy two examples of these statistics.

2 Why do you think the writer refers to so many of the difficulties and challenges that arose in making the film? Quote from the article in support of your answer.

WORD LEVEL WORK

Vocabulary

Dictionary and contextual work

Use a dictionary and the context of the passage to explain the meanings of the following words:

1 inconceivable	5 sequel	9 unprecedented
2 fluorescent	6 digital	10 simultaneously
3 authenticity	7 animation	11 labyrinthine
4 tendrils	8 concurrently	12 quizzically

Spelling

Silent 'k' word

Key words: **k**new   **k**nob   **k**nowledge

1 Use these key words in sentences of your own.

2 Learn these important silent 'k' words:

knife   **k**nives   **k**nee   **k**nit

knock   **k**not   **k**now

SENTENCE LEVEL WORK

Grammar and punctuation

Complex sentences

> *i*
>
> A *simple sentence* is made up of one main clause.
> A *compound sentence* is made up of two or more simple sentences joined by a conjunction, eg
>
> Simple sentence: *He's hurt.*
>
> Compound sentence: *He's hurt, but his reaction shows his confusion.*
>
> A *complex sentence* is made up of one main clause and one or more other clauses called *subordinate clauses*. Subordinate clauses do not make sense on their own, eg
>
> *'I would recognise it anywhere, but never supposed that I would find myself standing on the doorstep.'*
>
> Main clause: *'I would recognise it anywhere'*
> Subordinate clause: *'but never supposed that I would find myself standing on the doorstep.'*

Copy these complex sentences and underline the main clause in each one.

1 He decided to take a book along to pass the time and, at a thousand pages long, *The Lord of the Rings* was the perfect volume.

2 After reading just a few chapters, the young Jackson was lost among the wonders and terrors of Middle-earth.

3 We've arrived at the animation studio, and immediately Jackson is on the run, pounding up and down staircases and along labyrinthine corridors.

4 Hunching his shoulders, the director is miming how the troll should pluck out the spear and look at it quizzically as if it were a toothpick.

5 He repeats the pantomime, imitated by the animator.

TEXT LEVEL WORK

Writing

Non-fiction writing to recount – interview in a magazine article

> In the passage, which is an example of non-fiction writing to recount – magazine article, the writer uses particular conventions of layout. The language in the passage is also different from other types of writing, as a recount often uses the first person.

Language features

Conventions of layout – columns

When laying out magazine articles, writers and publishers often use columns. They do this to help the reader to scan and select those parts of the article that are of most interest, quickly and easily. Sometimes, as in the passage, the columns are separated by vertical lines.

Conventions of layout – illuminated capitals

One technique used by writers and publishers, to give a particular mood or impression to an article, is to use 'illuminated' lettering at the beginning of the passage. This elaborate and artistic technique was frequently used by monks in the middle ages and is often copied in writing which is historical or related to fantasy literature. In the passage, which relates to *The Lord of the Rings*, a fantasy trilogy, the illuminated capital reinforces the mood of the book.

Conventions of language – first person narrative

In this passage, the writer has chosen to use the first person for his recount, eg

> *'Yet, after travelling halfway round the world to Wellington, New Zealand, here I am outside Bag End, in Hobbiton.'*

Here, the use of the first person emphasises that the writer has a strong, personal connection with the subject and events that he is writing about, eg

> *'I would recognise it anywhere, but never supposed that I would find myself standing on the doorstep.'*

The first person also 'speaks' directly to the reader, so it helps them to feel involved.

Conventions of language – quotations and direct speech

The writer uses direct speech to give the reader a sense of being present at the events being described in the passage, eg

> *'"Let's talk as we go," he says.'*

The use of direct speech also lends credibility and authority to what the writer is saying, eg

> '"We've had an armourer working at an open forge crafting swords in the same way as they did in the Middle Ages," says Taylor.'

This impresses the reader with the efforts that the film-makers went to, to create an authentic atmosphere in the film.

Conventions of language – technical language

The writer uses technical vocabulary related to the world of cinema and film-making, eg

> 'cinema'; 'movies'; 'costume design'; 'scale layouts of the set'; 'animators'; 'digitally created'; 'special effects'; 'prosthetics'.

In addition to the technical vocabulary related to the world of cinema and film-making, the writer also uses language specific to the fantasy trilogy, *The Lord of the Rings*, on which the film is based. He refers to:

- individual characters from the novels, eg 'Bilbo Baggins and his cousin Frodo'; 'Gandalf'; 'King Theoden'
- types of characters from the novels, eg 'Orcs'; 'cave troll'; 'Uruk-hai warriors'; 'Elf'; 'wizard'; 'a Hobbit'
- places from the novels, eg 'Bag End', 'in Hobbiton', 'Helm's Deep', 'Lothlorien'
- objects from the novels, eg 'Longbottom Leaf, perhaps, or Old Toby'; 'stolen dragon-gold'; 'swords and spears and banners'.

Writing assignment

Imagine that you have interviewed one of the characters from *The Lord of the Rings* for a magazine article. Base your interview on one of the characters mentioned in the extract used in *Framework English Fiction Pupils' Book 2, Unit 4.2*. This passage is from Chapter 7, *The Mirror of Galadriel*, from *The Fellowship of the Ring*. Write the transcript of the interview, which describes the character's view of the events in the passage.

Use the information above, so that you carry out the correct conventions of layout and language.

Personal choice

Choose one of the following assignments.

1 Write the transcript of an interview with an actor, who played the part of one of the characters in the passage above.

2 Interview a character from a fairy tale or folk story, of your own choice.

During the Golden Age (1938–45) of comics, superheroes formed only a small segment of the total comic book market, other genres included: crime, western, romance, war, horror, and funny animals. The Silver Age (1956–69) was primarily a revival of superhero comic books. Many reasons have been suggested to explain this resurgence: nostalgia, anxieties about the communist threat from Russia and fears about the atomic age. In addition, superhero comics were flexible and easily adaptable to the tough, new regulations imposed in America by the _Comics Code Authority_. As a result, many of the other genres of comic books weakened, while the superheroes went from strength to strength.

I would argue that today, within the comic book media, with millions of issues published every year and many are now 'collectors' items' obtainable as back issues in comic shops and from specialist dealers. I think that the long-running characters, such as Superman, remain familiar to a wide audience because they often cross over from one medium to another. Thus, we have 'Superman – the Movie', with its sequels, and 'Superman – the TV series', with its spin-off, 'Smallville'.

Not all comic book genres were so fortunate. By comparison, two less popular comic book genres: cartoons and fantasy have fared differently. In my view, established cartoon material has been moderately successful. 'The Simpsons' and other Simpsons-related comic books have sold fairly well, but have been less successful than the TV show. Similarly, 'Beavis & Butthead' was a moderate hit, but failed to capture the qualities of the characters' TV voices, which undermined its effectiveness. All of these examples are from the 1990s, but when I look at any of the cartoon-based comic books of the past,

I see a more important factor. The problem is that when people lose interest in the cartoon, they will often cancel their subscriptions to the comic and the publishers run into financial problems. Only traditional cartoon characters, such as 'Mickey Mouse' or 'Donald Duck' have had lengthy runs, with the strength of the Disney empire helping to support them in the public consciousness.

I feel that fantasy comics based on previously established material have maintained a weak presence in the market. Marvel's 'Conan the Barbarian' lasted for 23 years but the various Conan spin-offs of the 1980s were less successful. 'Dungeons and Dragons' comics achieved a short-lived popularity, before being perceived as the haunt of 'geeks'. Yet, fantasy comics based on original material have done quite well, particularly those produced by independent companies. I would argue that original fantasy comics have achieved more success than their predecessors, when the authors actively promote their materials and are more responsive to their fans.

As for Super-heroines ...

Until the last decade, the majority of comic books were written by men, for men. Most women were, therefore, either romantic interests of the superhero or, alternatively, physically well-endowed sex symbols. Since the majority of comic books were produced by men, and catered for male interests, there were few comic books specifically about women. 'Wonder Woman' is one of the few surviving monthly series, that stars a female super-hero. It is amazing to think that 'Wonder Woman' has been going strong since 1942. No other female super-hero can compare to Wonder Woman's success or longevity. Wonder Woman is a success because, in my opinion, she has become a feminist icon.

I cannot abide those superheroines that merely 'ape' the behaviour of the long-established superheroes. Many female heroes that have had their own series were, unfortunately, copies of successful male heroes e.g. 'Supergirl' (1972–4) and 'Spider-Woman' (1978–83). These female imitations of established male super-heroes were ill-defined and unappealing. Worst of all, they were pale imitations of immature, macho, male attitudes, instead of promoting feminine strengths. Where were the superheroines with virtues, such as the ability to communicate feelings articulately, to show sensitivity, to work effectively in promoting teamwork? I, like many critics, would argue that feminism has yet to breach the male bastions of the comic book superhero!

However, some critics have argued that things have improved in the last decade for women in comics. Certainly, within the industry, the number of women involved in comic book production has increased with writers, artists, designers and editors often being female. Most teams of comic book heroes and heroines now have more than one female character, in order to be perceived as 'politically-correct'. Female super-heroes love, laugh, kill (or don't kill), and are hurt, maimed, or killed as regularly as their male counterparts. Yet, good quality comics with convincing female characters are still few and far between. Even in the late 1990s, the status of women in comics was still, by and large, not encouraging. One need only observe the current trend of overly-endowed, scantily clad, heroines in the media, such as Lara Croft and the popular 'Tomb Raider', to see the influence of modern superheroines. Popular or not, I fail to see how they are a step forward for women in comics. This should be a step in the right direction, with female characters being seen as heroic characters first, and female second but, sadly, women are still second-best in the comic book world!

Adapted from articles by Joel Grineau

TEXT LEVEL WORK

Comprehension

A 1 When was the 'Golden Age' of comics?

2 When was the 'Silver Age' of comics?

3 Which body imposed tough, new regulations on the publication of American comics?

4 Name two major, long-running, traditional cartoon characters.

5 Which of Marvel's superhero characters lasted 23 years, according to the article?

B 1 Why does the writer think that Wonder Woman has been such a successful and long-lived character?

2 Which two genres of comics does the writer consider to be 'less-popular' than the superheroes?

3 Explain the following in your own words:
   a *'resurgence'*
   b *'"ape" the behaviour'*
   c *'immature, macho, male attitudes'*.

4 What impression do you get of the relationship between TV and comics? Quote from the passage in support of your answer.

C 1 The writer of the second section of the passage seems critical of the majority of superheroines. Why do you think this is?

2 Why do you think that long-running, successful characters remain familiar to readers/audiences? Quote from the passage in support of your answer.

WORD LEVEL WORK

Vocabulary

Dictionary and contextual work

Comics
Use a dictionary and the context of the passage to explain the meaning of the following words:

1 genres	5 regulations	9 subscriptions
2 primarily	6 dominant	10 financial
3 nostalgia	7 familiar	11 predecessors
4 communist	8 medium	12 bastions

Spelling

Soft 'g' words
Key words: a**g**e   nostal**g**ia   dun**g**eon   resur**g**ence

1 Use these key words in sentences of your own.

2 Learn these important soft 'g' words:

ori**g**inal   **g**enre   ener**g**y   ima**g**ine

gender   strate**g**y   sta**g**e

SENTENCE LEVEL WORK

Grammar and punctuation

Paragraphing – topic sentences

Remember. A *paragraph* is a group of related sentences focusing on one topic. A *topic sentence* often begins a paragraph, giving an idea of what the subject is, eg

'I feel that fantasy comics based on previously established material have maintained a weak presence in the market.'

Here, the topic of the paragraph is the weakness of fantasy comics that tried to build on previously successful characters. The initial idea from the topic sentence is expanded, giving more detail, information or examples, eg

'Marvel's 'Conan the Barbarian' lasted for 23 years but the various Conan spin-offs of the 1980s were less successful.'

Copy and complete the table. For each sentence, suggest whether it is a topic sentence or additional detail, information or example.

Sentence	Topic/example
I would argue that superheroes are dominant today, within the comic book media, with millions of issues published every year and many are now 'collectors' items' obtainable as back issues in comic shops and from specialist dealers.	
Thus, we have 'Superman – the Movie', with its sequels, and 'Superman – the TV series', with its spin-off, 'Smallville'.	
Not all comic book genres were so fortunate.	
'The Simpsons' and other Simpsons-related comic books have sold fairly well, but have been less successful than the TV show.	
Until the last decade, the majority of comic books were written by men, for men.	
'Wonder Woman' is one of the few surviving monthly series, that stars a female super-hero.	
I cannot abide those superheroines that merely 'ape' the behaviour of the long-established superheroes.	
Many female heroes that have had their own series were, unfortunately, copies of successful male heroes eg 'Supergirl' (1972–4) and 'Spider-Woman' (1978–83).	
However, some critics have argued that things have improved in the last decade for women in comics.	
One need only observe the current trend of overly-endowed, scantily clad, heroines in the media, such as Lara Croft and the popular 'Tomb Raider', to see the influence of modern superheroines.	

TEXT LEVEL WORK

Writing

Persuasive writing – personal viewpoint

In persuasive writing, the writer tries to convince the reader to accept particular viewpoints, which the author may or may not agree with, personally. In this passage, the writer argues from a personal point of view, based on his own knowledge of the comic book genre.

Language features

Emphasis on key points
The writer puts emphasis on the important points by:

- using repetition, eg
    'comics, superheroes, superheroines'
- developing links in the argument, linking sentences at the ends and beginnings of paragraphs, eg
    '... superheroes went from strength to strength ...' Links to '... superheroes

are dominant, feminism has yet to breach the male bastions of the comic book superhero! ...' Links to '*... things have improved in the last decade for women in comics*'.

Emotive language

The writer makes his audience feel as if they are sharing the author's experiences. The language choices show that he is creating a particular impression. The writer stresses vocabulary that suggests a particular bias, with emotionally-loaded phrases and words designed to be positive about things the writer likes or agrees with, eg

'*strength to strength*'; '*actively promote their materials*'; '*responsive to their fans*'.

Other words and phrases are designed to be negative about those things the writer dislikes or disagrees with, eg

'*weakened*'; '*failed*'; '*weak*'; '*haunt of "geeks"*'.

Language to create tone

Sometimes the writer will use language in a particular way to create 'tones of voice', such as irony, where the words that the writer uses are different from his tone, eg

'*One need only observe the current trend of overly-endowed, scantily clad, heroines in the media, such as Lara Croft and the popular 'Tomb Raider', to see the influence of modern superheroines.*'

Taken literally, this suggests that superheroines are very successful and influential. However, the underlying tone suggests the exact opposite: that superheroines have not yet achieved the success and influence that they should have.

First person emphasis

Use of the first person makes it very clear that he has a strongly-held, personal view, eg

'*I think ... I see ... I feel ...*'.

The strength of the writer's expression sounds as if he believes what he is saying, eg

'*I would argue ... I cannot abide ... I fail to see ...*'.

Credibility

In order to carry authority, the writer creates the impression that what he is saying is 'official', eg

'*Golden Age (1938–45); Silver Age (1956–69)*'.

These are not the official names of the two periods of time, but give the impression that they are an agreed and authoritative title. Writers also refer to 'authority figures', in order to make their views seem important and right, eg

'*Comics Code Authority*'.

The writer has drawn attention to the 'authority figure' by making a hypertext link to another web page and underlining it.

Writing assignment

Write a persuasive personal article, either for, or against, fantasy films such as *Harry Potter*, *The Lord of the Rings* and *Batman*. You should consider whether:

- the films are acceptable because they show good overcoming evil and because they show violence in an unreal way
- the films are unacceptable because they do not show that evil sometimes overcomes good in real life
- the films are unacceptable because they encourage violence as being 'normal'.

Personal choice

Choose one of the following assignments.

1 Write an essay, with the title, 'It is a dangerous thing for young children to watch fantasy films and videos'.

2 Write a personal recount, in which you discuss the superheroes and superheroines that you know about. Do they seem to match the views of the writer of the passage?

There were eight.

THE SCHOOL DAYS OF AN INDIAN GIRL
Atlantic Monthly 85 (1900): 185–94.

THE LAND OF RED APPLES

There were eight in our party of bronzed children who were going East with the missionaries. Among us were three young braves, two tall girls, and we three little ones, Judewin, Thowin, and I.

We had been very impatient to start on our journey to the Red Apple Country, which, we were told, lay a little beyond the great circular horizon of the Western prairie. Under a sky of rosy apples we dreamt of roaming as freely and happily as we had chased the cloud shadows on the Dakota plains. We had anticipated much pleasure from a ride on the iron horse, but the throngs of staring palefaces disturbed and troubled us.

On the train, fair women, with tottering babies on each arm, stopped their haste and scrutinized the children of absent mothers. Large men, with heavy bundles in their hands, halted near by, and riveted their glassy blue eyes upon us.

I sank deep into the corner of my seat, for I resented being watched. Directly in front of me, children who were no larger than I hung themselves upon the backs of their seats, with their bold white faces toward me. Sometimes they took their forefingers out of their mouths and pointed at my moccasined feet. Their mothers, instead of reproving such rude curiosity, looked closely at me, and attracted their children's further notice to my blanket. This embarrassed me, and kept me constantly on the verge of tears.

I sat perfectly still, with my eyes downcast, daring only now and then to shoot long glances around me. Chancing to turn to the window at my side, I was quite breathless upon seeing one familiar object.

It was the telegraph pole which strode by at short paces. Very near my mother's dwelling, along the edge of a road thickly bordered with wild sunflowers, some poles like these had been planted by white men. Often I had stopped, on my way down the road, to hold my ear against the pole, and, hearing its low moaning, I used to wonder what the paleface had done to hurt it. Now I sat watching for each pole that glided by to be the last one.

In this way I had forgotten my uncomfortable surroundings, when I heard one of my comrades call out my name. I saw the missionary standing very near, tossing candies and gums into our midst. This amused us all, and we tried to see who could catch the most of the sweetmeats. The missionary's generous distribution of candies was impressed upon my memory by a disastrous result which followed. I had caught more than my share of candies and gums, and soon after our arrival at the school I had a chance to disgrace myself, which, I am ashamed to say, I did.

Though we rode several days inside of the iron horse, I do not recall a single thing about our luncheons.

It was night when we reached the school grounds. The lights from the windows of the large buildings fell upon some of the icicled trees that stood beneath them. We were led toward an open door, where the brightness of the lights within flooded out over the heads of the excited palefaces who blocked the way. My body trembled more from fear than from the snow I trod upon.

Entering the house, I stood close against the wall. The strong glaring light in the large whitewashed room dazzled my eyes. The noisy hurrying of hard shoes upon a bare wooden floor increased the whirring in my ears. My only safety seemed to be in keeping next to the wall.

As I was wondering in which direction to escape from all this confusion, two warm hands grasped me firmly, and in the same moment I was tossed high in midair. A rosy-cheeked paleface woman caught me in her arms. I was both frightened and insulted by such trifling. I stared into her eyes, wishing her to let me stand on my own feet, but she jumped me up and down with increasing enthusiasm. My mother had never made a plaything of her wee daughter. Remembering this I began to cry aloud.

They misunderstood the cause of my tears, and placed me at a white table loaded with food. There our party were united again. As I did not hush my crying, one of the older ones whispered to me, "Wait until you are alone in the night."

It was very little I could swallow besides my sobs, that evening.

"Oh, I want my mother and my brother Dawee! I want to go to my aunt!" I pleaded; but the ears of the palefaces could not hear me.

From the table we were taken along an upward incline of wooden boxes, which I learned afterward to call a stairway. At the top was a quiet hall, dimly lighted. Many narrow beds were in one straight line down the entire length of the wall. In them lay sleeping brown faces, which peeped just out of the coverings. I was tucked into bed with one of the tall girls, because she talked to me in my mother tongue and seemed to soothe me.

I had arrived in the wonderful land of rosy skies, but I was not happy, as I had thought I should be. My long travel and the bewildering sights had exhausted me. I fell asleep, heaving deep, tired sobs. My tears were left to dry themselves in streaks, because neither my aunt nor my mother was near to wipe them away.

Zitkala-sa

TEXT LEVEL WORK

Comprehension

A 1 How many children were in the group, travelling east?

2 Where had the children lived before their journey east?

3 What were the names of the three youngest children?

4 What was the name of the brother of the girl telling the story?

5 What '*lay a little beyond the great circular horizon of the Western prairie*'?

B 1 Explain why it is evident that the children arrived in the east, during winter.

2 What impression do you get of the attitudes of white children, from the point of view of the Native American children? Quote in support of your answer.

3 Explain the following in your own words:
   a '*a ride on the iron horse*'
   b '*instead of reproving such rude curiosity*'
   c '*disgrace myself*'
   d '*noisy hurrying of hard shoes*'.

4 What impression do you get of the relationship between the white people and the Native Americans? Quote in support of your answer.

C 1 Through the eyes of the girl in the story, how do white people seem? Find two examples of:

   a insensitivity towards the Native American children

   b attempts at kindness towards the Native American children.

2 Why do you think that the girl in the story refers to '*confusion*' and '*exhaustion*', in her account of her arrival in the east? Quote in support of your answer.

WORD LEVEL WORK

Vocabulary

Dictionary and contextual work

Use a dictionary and the context of the passage to explain the meanings of the following words:

1 horizon	5 dwelling	9 incline
2 prairie	6 missionary	10 bewildering
3 palefaces	7 sweetmeats	11 soothe
4 scrutinized	8 enthusiasm	12 trifling

Spelling

'aught' words

Key words: d**augh**ter   c**aught**

  1 Use these key words in sentences of your own.

  2 Learn these important 'aught' words:

    t**aught**   fr**aught**   h**augh**ty

    n**augh**ty   sl**augh**ter

SENTENCE LEVEL WORK

Grammar and punctuation

Complex sentences – subordinate clauses

Remember. A *complex sentence* is made up of a *main clause* and a dependent, *subordinate clause*. The main clause is independent and can stand alone, as a simple sentence. A subordinate clause cannot form a complete sentence by itself. A subordinate clause needs a main clause to complete the sentence, so it is sometimes called a dependent clause, eg

  Complex sentence: '*There were eight in our party of bronzed children who were going East with the missionaries.*'

  Main clause: '*There were eight in our party of bronzed children*'
  Subordinate clause: '*who were going East with the missionaries.*'

Subordinate clauses may come anywhere in a sentence.

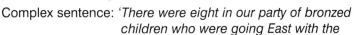

Copy these complex sentences and underline the subordinate clause in each one.

1   It was the telegraph pole which strode by at short paces.

2   Now I sat watching for each pole that glided by to be the last one.

3   It was night when we reached the school grounds.

4   We had been very impatient to start on our journey to the Red Apple Country, which, we were told, lay a little beyond the great circular horizon of the Western prairie.

5   Remembering this I began to cry aloud.

TEXT LEVEL WORK

Writing

Contrast in personal recount

In a personal recount, writers usually describe events that they have experienced and record how they felt about them. Often, the writer will compare the similarities and the differences of their situation before, and the situation they are in, now.

Language features

Figurative language

One of the key language features in this personal recount, is the contrast between the Native American girl's previous life and her new life in *The Land of Red Apples*. In the passage, the writer contrasts many different aspects of the girl's experiences, exaggerating some and playing down others.

Figurative language can be used for a number of purposes. One of its main uses is to describe things in a very vivid way. Another is to compare things that are not usually associated with one another, as a way of sharing with the reader how the girl sees things.

Describing

When describing the experiences of the girl in the passage, the writer uses metaphors to create vivid and unusual associations of ideas and convey an impression of the characters and their attitudes.

Sharing viewpoints

The writer tries to give the reader an insight into how the Native Americans tried to describe things about the white man's way of life that were alien to them, eg

   '*... telegraph pole which strode by at short paces ...*'

contains a personification and a metaphor to describe the telegraph poles that the train is passing. The girl uses a personification to describe the poles as striding past the window. A metaphor is used to show the speed of the train passing the poles, which appear to pass quickly '*at short paces*'.

   '*the iron horse*' is a metaphor to describe steam trains
   '*palefaces*' is a metaphor to describe the white people.

Changing atmosphere

Initial expectations

Writing in the first person, the writer uses the metaphor, '*sky of rosy apples*', to give a sense of the warm, sweet, summer feelings that the girl and her companions hoped to experience. She establishes, from a clear, personal viewpoint, the high hopes of the children, eg

'We had been very impatient to start on our journey to the Red Apple Country ...'
'... we dreamt of roaming as freely and happily ...'
'We had anticipated much pleasure ...'.

Change in atmosphere

After giving the impression that the children were looking forward to the trip, the writer describes how things start to go wrong on the train, eg

'... throngs of staring palefaces disturbed and troubled us ...'.

Expectations of behaviour

The writer is successful in communicating the differences between the way that the Native Americans had been brought up by their parents and the attitudes of the 'palefaces'. The Native American girl feels that the 'palefaces' are very rude to stare at them, eg

'... riveted their glassy blue eyes upon us.'

The girl clearly expects paleface adults to tell their children not to be rude, as they would have in Native American families, eg

'Their mothers, instead of reproving such rude curiosity, looked closely at me ...'.

Conveying emotions through physical description

The writer conveys the contrasts in the situation and the expectations by stating the feelings of the Native American girl, eg

'I resented being watched ...'
'This embarrassed me, and kept me constantly on the verge of tears.'

Her feelings are reinforced by the physical descriptions that the writer uses, eg

'I sank deep into the corner ...'; 'I sat perfectly still, with my eyes downcast ...';
'My body trembled ...'; '... dazzled my eyes ...'; '... whirring in my ears ...'.

Through these physical details, the writer conveys the dejection, strangeness and isolation that the girl experienced.

Writing assignment

Write a personal recount about an experience in your own life, when you started out with high hopes, only to find that things going wrong distressed you. Use the information above to help you. You should consider how you could convey the contrast through:

- figurative language
- first person recount of how your understanding of the situation was different from those of the people around you
- changes in atmosphere or mood
- expectations of behaviour
- description of physical detail.

Personal choice

Choose one of the following assignments.

1 Write a first person description of the same events, from the point of view of the *Missionary* mentioned in the passage.

2 Write a third person description of the Native American girl, as she would have appeared to the palefaces on the train.

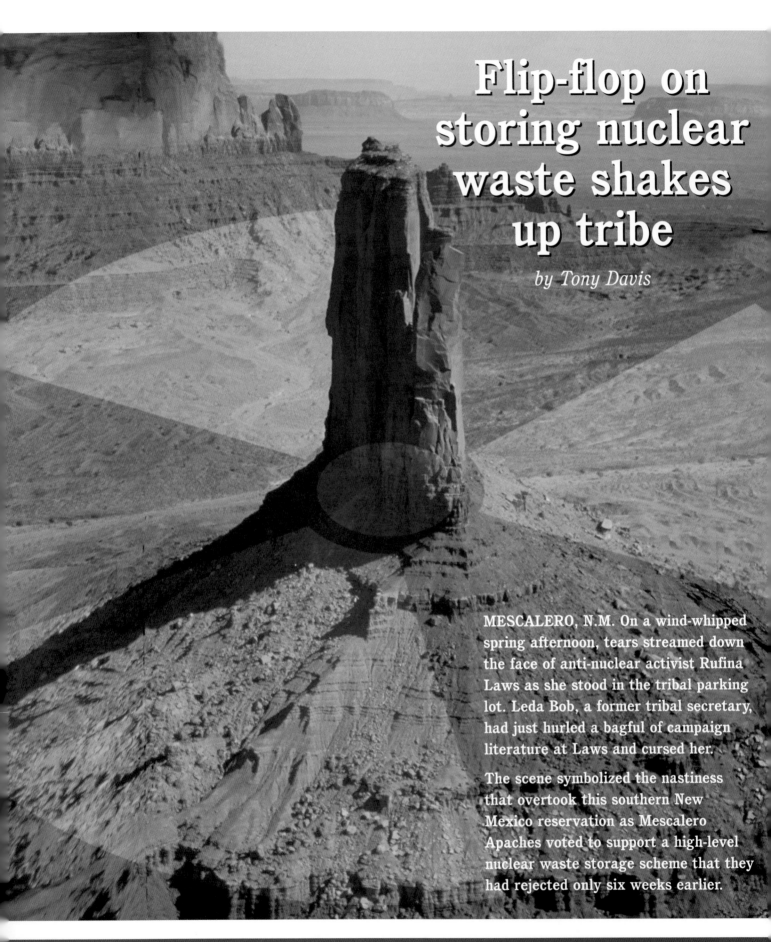

Flip-flop on storing nuclear waste shakes up tribe

by Tony Davis

MESCALERO, N.M. On a wind-whipped spring afternoon, tears streamed down the face of anti-nuclear activist Rufina Laws as she stood in the tribal parking lot. Leda Bob, a former tribal secretary, had just hurled a bagful of campaign literature at Laws and cursed her.

The scene symbolized the nastiness that overtook this southern New Mexico reservation as Mescalero Apaches voted to support a high-level nuclear waste storage scheme that they had rejected only six weeks earlier.

The reversal was the tribal equivalent of a steamroller. As leaders barraged the tribe's 3,300 members with letters, the divisive campaign split both families and friends, leaving bitterness that could take months or years to heal. The plan that members approved calls for the tribe to store 40,000 tons of lead-shielded, spent fuel rods from nuclear power plants owned by 33 electric utilities.

Supporters of the storage had been dumbfounded by a 490–361 'no' vote at a Jan. 31 referendum... Until then, few Mescaleros had spoken openly against 30-year president Wendell Chino, one of the country's most powerful Indian leaders. Suddenly, Laws, who had gone door-to-door to round up opposition, became an international celebrity in the anti-nuclear movement. She drew interviews from British and German newspapers and planned a national speaking tour.

Then, tribal housing director Fred Kaydahzinne garnered 200 signatures in a petition drive to hold a second referendum. He said 'misinformation' about safety issues threatened a project promising 300 to 500 jobs and $250 million in benefits.

The biggest sparks flew over charges that petition-gatherers had promised $2,000 dividends if the referendum passed. Five Mescaleros told the Albuquerque Tribune that they'd personally heard such promises. Tribal leaders strongly denied that charge and blasted critics as dupes of Greenpeace and other Anglo environmental groups.

They accused Laws of mismanaging the tribe's Head Start program when she was director three years ago, although federal documents show that the program was already out of compliance with federal rules when Laws took over.

In letters, leaders promised that the radioactive rods would not leak and that their lead storage casks would never be opened on the reservation.

"Do you honestly think your council whom you have elected would consider something that could be harmful to themselves and their own people?" asked one tribal letter. "Some of the council may be related to some of you. The council, vice president and president have family, relatives and friends who care a great deal about them and feel badly when they are accused so falsely."

As they left the polls in early March, many 'yes' voters said they were moved by the promise of better schools. Currently, the reservation has only an elementary school, and many Mescaleros say their children are victims of prejudice in off-reservation schools.

"For the first time the Mescaleros have the upper hand," said Zachary Begay, a patroller at the tribe's ski resort. "It's been a long time since Indian people have had a leverage against surrounding communities."

Most New Mexico leaders opposed the project, but several bills that would have banned or regulated it died in the legislature. Although Mescaleros say Indian sovereignty would stop enforcement of a ban, state Attorney General Tom Udall has vowed to watchdog the project's push for federal licensing.

"I think this idea of moving this kind of waste all across the country to only a so-called temporary facility is ill-conceived," Udall said.

Laws, 50, said she felt the fight was worth it, because it publicly exposed the tribal leadership's iron grip. But she says she'll retreat from the battle lines, set up a nuclear information center and let others do the organizing.

"The only thing I can do now is raising consciousness on this issue," Laws said, "not only for New Mexicans but for as many people as possible."

"For the first time the Mescaleros have the upper hand"

TEXT LEVEL WORK

Comprehension

A 1 Which tribe of Native Americans found itself caught up in the dispute about nuclear waste?

 2 Where does the tribe live?

 3 How many Native Americans are in the tribe?

 4 What is the name of the Native American woman who became a celebrity during the campaign?

 5 What is the name of the state Attorney General who would scrutinise the project?

B 1 Explain the following in your own words:
  a '*anti-nuclear activist*'
  b '*tribal parking lot*'
  c '*victims of prejudice in off-reservation schools*'.

 2 Why do you think that the campaign split the tribe? Quote in support of your answer.

 3 The Native American woman quoted at the end of the passage sees only one thing left for her to do. What is that?

 4 Explain why campaigners were concerned about '*misinformation*'. Quote in support of your answer.

C 1 The anti-nuclear campaigners used various tactics to build up opposition to the project. Explain at least two strategies that they used.

 2 How does the writer of the article make use of statistics/data in reporting the situation?

  • In what ways are these statistics convincing?
  • In what ways do they fail to convince?

WORD LEVEL WORK

Vocabulary

Dictionary and contextual work
Use a dictionary and the context of the passage to explain the meanings of the following words:

1 campaign	5 divisive	9 international
2 reservation	6 utilities	10 celebrity
3 equivalent	7 dumbfounded	11 garnered
4 barraged	8 referendum	12 dividends

Spelling

'ment' words
Key words: enforce**ment**   ele**ment**ary   environ**ment**al

 1 Use these key words in sentences of your own.

 2 Learn these important 'ment' words:

  develop**ment**   move**ment**   docu**ment**ary   govern**ment**

  settle**ment**   involve**ment**   argu**ment**ative

SENTENCE LEVEL WORK

Grammar and punctuation

Reported or indirect speech

If you want to tell someone what another person said, you can use *reported speech*, or *indirect speech*. In reported or indirect speech, the precise *meaning* of the speaker's words is given, but the exact words are not directly quoted. Reported speech is usually used to talk about the past, so we normally change the tense of the words spoken, eg

> *'He said 'misinformation' about safety issues <u>threatened</u> a project promising 300 to 500 jobs and $250 million in benefits.'*

Reported speech, or indirect speech begins with a clause that includes a *reporting verb*. We use reporting verbs like 'say', 'tell', 'ask', and we may use the word 'that' to introduce the reported words. Inverted commas, or speech marks, are not used, eg

> *'Laws, 50, said she felt the fight was worth it, because it publicly exposed the tribal leadership's iron grip.'*

To convert direct speech into indirect speech:
When changing from direct speech to indirect speech, it is often necessary to change the pronouns to match the subject of the sentence, eg

> Direct speech: *'"<u>We</u> have, personally, heard such promises," the five Mescaleros told the Albuquerque Tribune.'*

> Reported speech: Five Mescaleros told the Albuquerque Tribune that <u>they'd</u> personally heard such promises.

Change each of these examples of direct speech into reported speech.

1. "Do you honestly think your council whom you have elected would consider something that could be harmful to themselves and their own people?" asked one tribal letter.

2. "Some of the council may be related to some of you. The council, vice president and president have family, relatives and friends who care a great deal about them and feel badly when they are accused so falsely," stated the same tribal letter.

3. "For the first time the Mescaleros have the upper hand," said Zachary Begay, a patroller at the tribe's ski resort. "It's been a long time since Indian people have had a leverage against surrounding communities."

4. "I think this idea of moving this kind of waste all across the country to only a so-called temporary facility is ill-conceived," Udall said.

5. "The only thing I can do now is raising consciousness on this issue," Laws said, "not only for New Mexicans but for as many people as possible."

TEXT LEVEL WORK

Writing

Newspaper report

> This passage is a newspaper report, also published on the Internet. It makes use of many of the conventions of layout, which are familiar to readers of newspapers: headlines, photographs and by-lines. Newspapers and Internet articles are also characterised by a range of language features: figurative language, emotive language, bias, quotations from interviews and the use of data.

Language features

Figurative language

The writer makes use of figurative language, such as metaphors, in order to make the writing more vivid and effective, eg

> *'wind-whipped'; 'steamroller'; 'The biggest sparks flew'.*

Emotive language

The writer uses emotive language to encourage the reader to feel or respond in a particular way. He uses negative words and phrases when he wishes the reader to oppose a certain view. For example, the opening paragraph is designed to make the reader feel sympathy for Rufina Laws, when she is the victim of an assault:

> *'... tears streamed down the face of anti-nuclear activist Rufina Laws ...'.*

Again, when he wishes the reader to agree with him, the writer carefully chooses words and phrases that are emotionally-loaded, eg

> *'... the divisive campaign split both families and friends, leaving bitterness that could take months or years to heal ...'.*

Here, words such as 'divisive', 'split' and 'bitterness' are used to manipulate the reader's responses. Similarly, he uses positive words and phrases, when he wishes the reader to support a view, eg

> *'"I think this idea of moving this kind of waste all across the country to only a so-called temporary facility is ill-conceived," Udall said.'*

Here, the writer uses words and phrases such as 'so-called' and 'ill-conceived' to make the reader feel that the idea of moving nuclear waste across the country is a bad idea.

Bias

The writer's use of emotive words and phrases means that his language is not intended to be objective and neutral, it is designed to manipulate the reader's reactions – it is biased, rather than factual, eg

> *'Most New Mexico leaders opposed the project, but several bills that would have banned or regulated it died in the legislature.'*

> *'Although Mescaleros say Indian sovereignty would stop enforcement of a ban, state Attorney General Tom Udall has vowed to watchdog the project's push for federal licensing.'*

The use of the word 'watchdog' is not factual, it is almost threatening.

Quotations

The writer uses quotations, in order to show the opposing viewpoints, eg

'*"Do you honestly think your council whom you have elected would consider something that could be harmful to themselves and their own people?"'*

This was written in a tribal letter, yet another view was quoted in order to counteract it, eg

'*"For the first time the Mescaleros have the upper hand ..."'*.

Data

The writer makes use of data and statistics to sound more convincing to the reader, eg

'*As leaders barraged the tribe's 3,300 members with letters ...*';
'*... 40,000 tons of lead-shielded, spent fuel rods from nuclear power plants ...*'.

Such data sounds impressive and it makes the writer seem knowledgeable about the subject.

Writing assignment

In the passage, there is a clear idea that the Mescalero Indians are regarded as 'second-class' citizens, by some politicians. They are at a disadvantage in opposing government policies. Imagine that you are a journalist. A meeting has been arranged about moving the Mescalero Indians from their homelands onto reservations, against their will. Write a newspaper report about the meeting. You should consider the conventions of writing a newspaper report:

- Layout – headlines, photographs or illustrations, columns etc.
- Language – figurative and emotive language, bias, quotations, data.

Personal choice

Choose one of the following assignments.

1 Write the speech that the Mescalero chief might make, arguing against the tribe being moved from their homelands.

2 Write the speech that the Attorney General might make, arguing that it is in the interests of the tribe to live on a reservation.

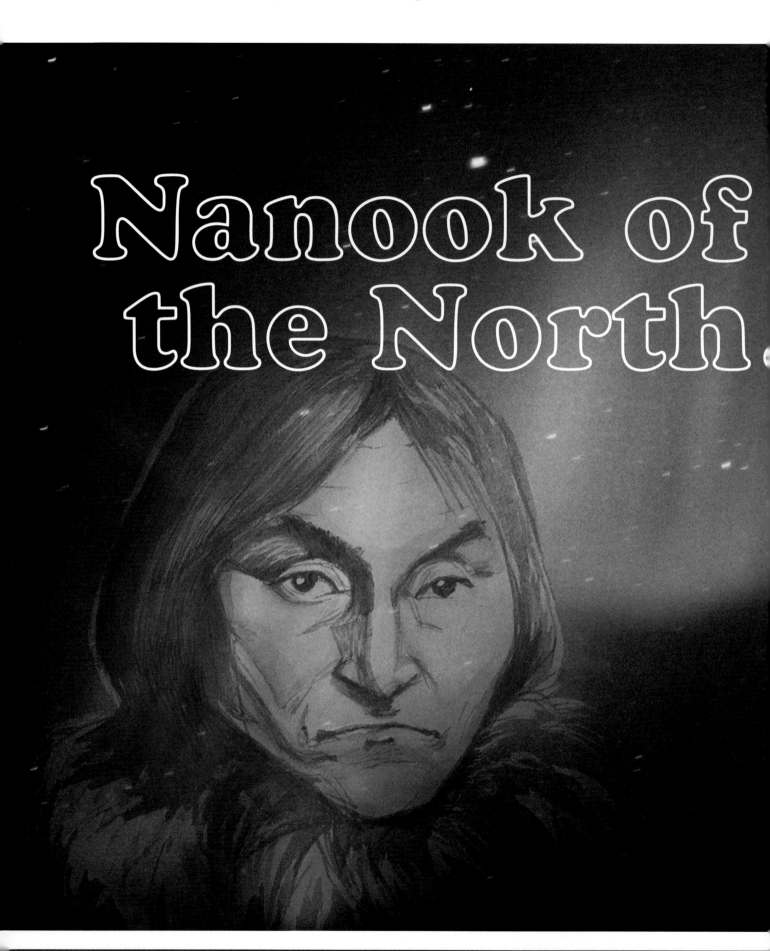

Nanook of the North.

In the 1920s and 1930s, the documentary film Nanook of the North *became famous throughout the world. It showed the traditional life of the Inuit Native Americans in the Arctic. The star of the film was an Inuit called Alakarialak, who played Nanook. The cinematographer, Robert Flaherty, became a famous film-maker, while Nanook died of starvation, on a hunting expedition, two years after making the film.*

In this personal recount a modern Inuit is trying to establish whether the man who played Nanook was his relative.

The hunting scenes were staged and much of the film makes present-day Inuit audiences roar with laughter, but Robert Flaherty's *Nanook of the North* is one of the earliest filmed records of the traditional life-style of Inuit. Unfortunately, no one kept track of who the Inuit actors in the film were. Moses Nowkawalk of Inukjuak, Quebec, had to do years of research to establish the identity of Nanook – thought by some people to have been Moses' grandfather.

"It started when I first saw *Nanook of the North* in school," says Moses. "As we were watching it we laughed because it was funny, especially when he was trying to pull that bearded seal through the ice. As it turned out, that scene was faked. They had made two holes and had several men pulling a rope to make it look like he was having a fight with the seal."

A teacher in Inukjuak, George Divecky (who is now superintendent of education for the Keewatin), used to interview people on the history of the community. He noted that Moses' grandfather was called Alakarialak, the same name as the actor playing Nanook in the film. But not all the people he interviewed agreed that Nanook was Moses' grandfather; some said there were two Alakarialaks. Showing the movie in the community didn't end the controversy. Moses' grandfather had died around 1927 and the actor who portrayed Nanook died about the same time. Even Moses' father couldn't solve the puzzle as he had been only four years old at the time.

"A few years ago, an old man from Akulivik went on the radio saying that he used to live around here when he was a kid. He was about 10 years old around 1920 when the film was made," said Moses. The old man said he saw Flaherty and Alakarialak make the movie, and later told Moses' father that 'Nanook' had two sisters named Mava and Mary. As Moses' father had two aunts with the same names, for a time the case was considered closed – Nanook was indeed Moses' grandfather.

More evidence mounted. Photographs taken of Nanook by Flaherty showed that Alakarialak was a 'dead ringer' for Adamie Inukpuk, a cousin of Moses. When Moses came to Ottawa, he met Monica Flaherty, Robert's daughter, and obtained more photographs of Nanook to show elders in Great Whale River, Inukjuak, Povungnituk and Akulivik. The results of showing the photographs were inconclusive. "One man in Povungnituk, Markoosie, was just the right age and had seen all these people, but he just couldn't see. Another woman in Povungnituk was senile. As it turned out this research should have been done in the 1940s or '50s.

"I figured that some controversy or doubt remained," says Moses, "and I decided to solve it once and for all by doing something I should have done earlier – look in the church records." The official records for Inukjuak were kept in Great Whale and then had been sent to George River and couldn't be found. From the minister's own records, however, Moses discovered a Daniel Alakarialak, whose wife was named Hannah, and who had two sons, Joanassie and Samson. Moses has an uncle called Samson.

I flipped through the pages and didn't find anything about another Alakarialak. My grandfather was Daniel and as I went through more of the records I saw that Daniel Alakarialak died of tuberculosis on September 11, 1927. Other records showed the man in the movie died two years after Flaherty left in 1921. Flaherty said in his books that the man in the movie died of starvation. That would have been in 1923 and my grandfather died in 1927. That clarified the whole situation for me, finally. The man in the movie was not my grandfather.

'Search for Nanook,' Inuktitut, Ottawa: Indian and Northern Affairs, Winter 1984.
Courtesy of INUKTITUT Archives

TEXT LEVEL WORK

Comprehension

A 1 What is the name of the person who played the part of Nanook, in the film?

   2 What was the name of the film-maker who produced the film of *Nanook*?

   3 What was the name of the Native American, who carried out research to establish the identity of Nanook?

   4 Of what disease did Daniel Alakarialak die on September 11, 1927?

   5 What were the names of Daniel Alakarialak's wife and two sons?

B 1 Explain why you think that the Native American audiences roared with laughter, when they saw Robert Flaherty's film *Nanook of the North*?

   2 Calculate in which year the real Alakarialak died, according to Robert Flaherty's book. Explain what caused the death of the real Alakarialak.

   3 Name three places amongst those visited by the researchers, seeking to establish the identity of the real Alakarialak.

   4 Explain the following in your own words:
     a *'cinematographer'*
     b *'recount'*
     c *'Inuit'*
     d *'dead ringer'*.

C 1 Why do you think that Robert Flaherty would have had to fake some of the hunting scenes in the film of *Nanook*? Explain why this would not necessarily undermine the value of the film.

   2 Explain why you think it was so difficult for the researchers to establish the identity of the real Nanook. Quote in support of your answer.

WORD LEVEL WORK

Vocabulary

Dictionary and contextual work

Use a dictionary and the context of the passage to explain the meanings of the following words:

1 documentary	5 faked	9 history
2 traditional	6 scene	10 community
3 research	7 superintendent	11 evidence
4 identity	8 interview	12 senile

Spelling

'or' words

Key words: p**or**trayed   rec**or**ds   hist**ory**   act**or**

1 Use these key words in sentences of your own.

2 Learn these important 'or' words:

narrat**or**   auth**or**   maj**ority**   auth**ority**

min**or**   trait**or**   curs**or**   direct**ory**

SENTENCE LEVEL WORK

Grammar and punctuation

Standard English – dialect and register

Remember. A *dialect* is defined by a geographical region or ethnic group, such as the Inuit, Native Americans, who live in the Arctic areas.

A *register* is based on an activity or occupation, such as a group of people who have a common employment or interest and who use specialist language in their day-to-day work. They usually use a similar vocabulary and expressions to reinforce the group identity. They also exclude people who do not belong to the group.

In the passage, there are examples of both dialect and register.

Dialect: Inukjuak   specific geographical name   dialect vocabulary

Register: star   person famous in film industry   occupational

Copy and complete the table. Write down whether the references given in the table may be defined as examples of dialect or of register, or of both. The first one has been done for you.

Word	Feature	Reason	Type
movie	American vocabulary for film	Occupation + geography	Dialect + register
Povungnituk			
radio			
kid			
cinematographer			
Keewatin			
dead ringer			
scene			
George River			
photographs			
Great Whale			
actors			

TEXT LEVEL WORK

Writing

Report based on personal recount

> In the passage, the writer is writing a personal recount of research that he carried out. The recount is a summary of his search for the truth.

Language features

Research

Moses Nowkawalk of Inukjuak, Quebec, had to do years of research to establish the identity of Nanook. Amongst the evidence that he had to find, he:

- interviewed people
- showed the film to the Inuit community
- obtained photographs
- met Monica Flaherty, Robert's daughter
- tried to trace official church records
- had access to the minister's own records.

Establishing the facts

Legends are based on truth, but the truth has become clouded by a lack of factual evidence or confusion about the facts that are known. Starting with the legend of Nanook, what did the writer know?

- the film was made in 1921
- the actor who played Nanook was called Alakarialak
- the man in the movie died of starvation, on a hunting expedition, in 1923.

Context of the research

Any research is set in a specific context. What is the truth that is being sought? Where is the evidence? What does the evidence tell us? In the case of Moses Nowkawalk, the quest was to establish the identity of Nanook.

Such research provides its own difficulties:

- the film was made over 60 years before
- no one kept track of who the Inuit actors in the film were
- not all the people he interviewed agreed that Nanook was Moses' grandfather
- some said there were two Alakarialaks
- Moses' grandfather had died around 1927 and the actor who portrayed Nanook died about the same time
- 'Nanook' had two sisters named Mava and Mary, and Moses' father had two aunts with the same names
- photographs taken of Nanook by Flaherty showed that Alakarialak was a *'dead ringer'* for Adamie Inukpuk, a cousin of Moses
- one witness was blind, another was senile
- the research needed to have been done in the 1940s or 50s
- the official records for Inukjuak were kept in Great Whale and then had been sent to George River and couldn't be found.

The difficulty, then, with any research, is how to find the evidence. Is it still in existence? Is it accurate? What conclusions can be drawn from the evidence that you *do* have?

Effect on the audience
Legends usually involve a mystery, caused by the inconclusive nature of the evidence. They often involve a tragedy of some kind, such as the death of Alakarialak of starvation, two years after making the film. This has the effect of intriguing the reader and engaging their interest in the search for the truth.

Conflicts and confusions
Sometimes, the legend gathers conflicting evidence or confusing elaborations, as time passes. The legend of Nanook was no different:

- the actor and Moses' grandfather died at around the same time
- 'Nanook' had two sisters named Mava and Mary, and Moses' father had two aunts with the same names
- there were two Alakarialaks
- official records couldn't be found
- several Inuits looked similar in photographs
- the results of showing the photographs were inconclusive.

Writing assignment
Research different sources (books, CD-Roms, Internet) and make notes about the legend of the Native American princess, Pocahontas, and her love for the paleface, John Smith.

Record which sources you use and acknowledge those sources in your report. In your note-taking, use diagrams, abbreviations etc.

Write your findings as a personal recount of your researches, including:

- establishing the facts
- context
- effects on the reader
- conflicts and confusions.

Personal choice

Choose one of the following assignments.

1 Write the truth about the legend of Pocahontas, from her own point of view.

2 Write the truth about the legend of Pocahontas, from John Smith's point of view.

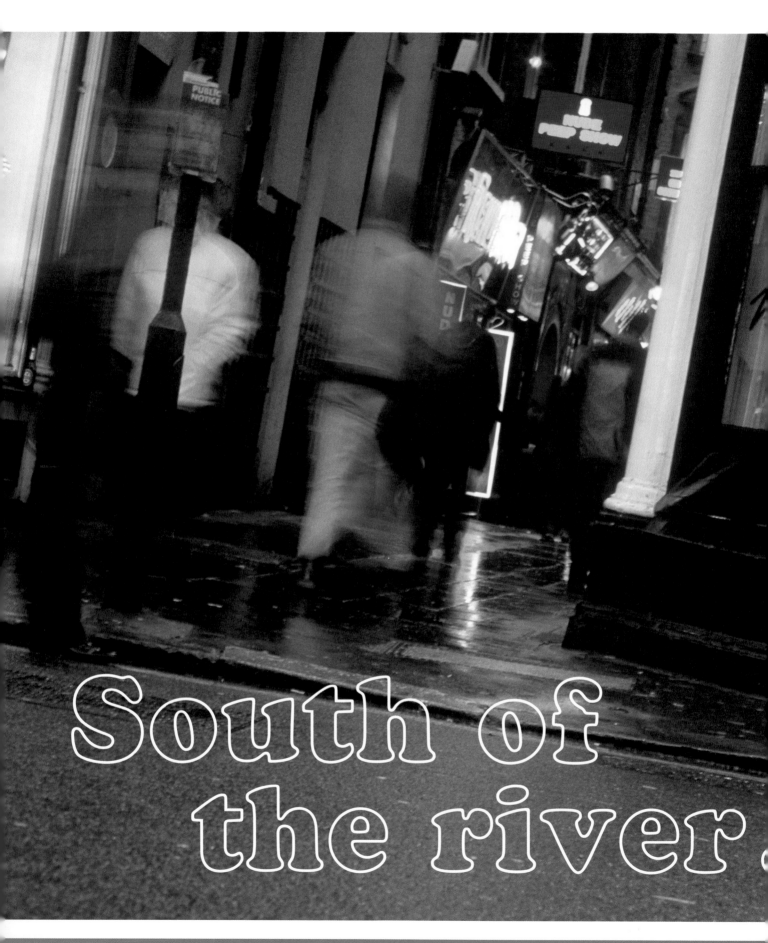

South of
the river.

A CurtainUp London Review
The Villains' Opera

By Lizzie Loveridge

John Gay's *The Beggars' Opera* was a phenomenal success in 1728 when it was staged by John Rich in London's Lincoln's Inn Fields. It was said then that, 'It made Gay rich and Rich gay'. It was famously updated by Berthold Brecht and Kurt Weill in 1928 as *The Threepenny Opera*, a difficult act to follow. In January, I saw a modern rock version at the Young Vic Studio called *Soho Story*. Now our revered National Theatre brings us *The Villains' Opera*, reworking some of the original tunes into a modern musical. The characters are the gun wielding, drug dealing modern equivalents of Gay's lower class of cut-throats, whores and highwaymen.

Set in southeast London on the 'wrong side of the water' (south of the Thames) to the backdrop of The Dome and Canary Wharf, at Woolwich, is the pub, 'The Flower of Kent' run by Peachum, a small time police informer and criminal wheeler dealer. Mr Big, the gangland boss lives away from the crime areas in a pretty village in Kent as a respectable member of society. Captain Macheath is a criminal with ambition, a persistent womaniser, he has married Polly Peachum and got Lucy Lockit in the family way. Lucy's father, is a bent copper (a policeman who takes back-handers). Lockit needs a name to arrest and Peachum gives him Macheath whom he doesn't know has married his daughter. We follow the villains through their underworld, gangs of car thieves, street criminals and lapdancers in Soho vice clubs as Peachum and Lockit attempt to catch Macheath, who later uncovers Mr Big's pot of gold and turns a policewoman to the dark side.

Nick Dear's script is full of colourful language and references to local places in the seamier side of London. He has created a realistic picture that's often not funny but full of irony. These are menacing men who treat their women, wives and daughters badly. Pretty tunes sit next to ugly lyrics. We have Mrs Peachum singing 'I Love My Man' about how much she loves her husband, the man who regularly batters her or 'Street Crime', a song celebrating mugging and car theft. Although Dear concentrates on the criminal classes, he also portrays the homeless and some of the affluent villagers who want Mr Big to stand for election to the parish council. I liked Stephen Warbeck's music. It is a mixture of rock and rock ballads, some using Gay's tunes.

Tim Supple, a director known for his innovative, physical productions at the Young Vic and the Royal Shakespeare Company, has created a Mayfair nightclub scene that is so realistic you almost feel that you're watching a live porn show. The girls strutting their bodies in a raunchy dance, singing 'Visa, Mastercard, Amex ...', turn out to be aspiring actresses and students of medicine, using the club to pay school fees. Robert Innes Hopkins' ten dramatic sets use a backdrop of rolling metal doors, the sky often lit up with local landmarks – the highlights being an East Greenwich Tube Station and a motorway driving scene.

The musical is not sung through and many of the performers are National Theatre ensemble actors who can also sing, which makes for high quality performances. Alexander Hanson has the right amount of feckless charm as Macheath. Madeleine Worrall and Elizabeth Renihan sing well as Macheath's girlfriends; Beverley Klein excels as Mrs Peachum belting out her songs. There are many good cameos of gangsters and petty thieves.

The final shoot out is well staged, comprehensive and played for laughs. Some of the spoken humour needs local knowledge to be appreciated but the accents are accessible. I couldn't recommend that you take the under 18s to this show with its lavish helpings of sex and violence. The three hours are well paced, with plenty to laugh at and several tunes one would like to hear again.

© 2000 Elyse Sommer, *CurtainUp*

TEXT LEVEL WORK

Comprehension

A 1 Who wrote *The Beggars' Opera*?

2 Who wrote *The Threepenny Opera*?

3 Where does *The Villains' Opera* take place?

4 In which year was *The Beggars' Opera* first successful?

5 Where does Mr Big live?

B 1 Explain the following in your own words:

a '*It was famously updated ...*'
b '*... wrong side of the water ....*'
c '*... seamier side ...*'.

2 Why do you think that the production might not be suitable for anyone under the age of 18?

3 What evidence is there that the production is a successful combination of humour and violence?

4 Why do you think that the production would be particularly popular with people living in southeast London?

C 1 Why do you think that Nick Dear's script is reviewed as being full of contrasts and contradictions?

2 How has the National Theatre modernised the previous successful versions of the musical?

WORD LEVEL WORK

Vocabulary

Dictionary and contextual work

Use a dictionary and the context of the passage to explain the meanings of the following words:

1 revered	5 menacing	9 innovative
2 highwaymen	6 lyrics	10 landmarks
3 wharf	7 affluent	11 ensemble
4 persistent	8 ballads	12 cameos

Spelling

'ie' words

Key words: w**ie**lding   thi**e**ves

1 Use these key words in sentences of your own.

2 Learn these important 'ie' words:

bel**ie**ve   rev**ie**w   misch**ie**f   rel**ie**f

br**ie**f   ach**ie**ve   prev**ie**w

SENTENCE LEVEL WORK

Grammar and punctuation

Standard English

> Standard English is not superior over any other dialect. Regional dialects in the UK, and the English-speaking world, have huge local support and are vitally important to local cultures. They are often more important to individuals than standard English.
>
> The differences between standard English and other regional dialects are usually in grammar and vocabulary, eg
>
> regional dialect: 'small time'
>
> standard English: 'unimportant, petty, trivial'.

Copy and complete the table. Translate the dialect words into standard English.

Regional dialect	Standard English
wheeler-dealer	
in the family way	
gangland	
bent	
copper	
back-handers	
lapdancers	
mugging	
raunchy	
feckless	
belting out	
shoot out	

TEXT LEVEL WORK

Writing

Theatre review

> In this passage, the writer begins by putting the production into its historical context. Next, she provides a summary of the main story, known as a *synopsis*. Following this, she concentrates on the details of this specific production. Finally, she gives the reader a conclusion, in which she sums up her opinions of the musical.

Language features

Context

The writer begins the passage by giving the reader an overview of the origins of the musical. She draws attention to the original version of the musical, John Gay's *The Beggars' Opera*. Next, she refers to its successor, 200 years later, Brecht and Weill's *The Threepenny Opera*. Then, she mentions the modern rock version at the Young Vic Studio called *Soho Story*. Finally, she states the production that she is reviewing:

> '*National Theatre brings us* The Villains' Opera, *reworking some of the original tunes into a modern musical.*'

In the opening paragraph, the writer has put the production being reviewed into its full context, so that the reader has a fuller understanding of the background.

Synopsis

The writer follows the context paragraph with a summary of the main plot, or storyline.

- She explains the setting, eg

  > '*Set in southeast London on the 'wrong side of the water' (south of the Thames) to the backdrop of The Dome and Canary Wharf, at Woolwich, is the pub, 'The Flower of Kent'.*'

- The writer introduces the main characters and their roles, eg

  > '*Peachum, a small time police informer and criminal wheeler dealer. Mr Big, the gangland boss ...*'
  > '*Captain Macheath is a criminal with ambition ...*'
  > '*Lucy's father, is a bent copper (a policeman who takes back-handers)*'.

- The relationships between the characters are also explained, eg

  > '*Captain Macheath ... has married Polly Peachum and got Lucy Lockit in the family way ...*'
  > '*Lockit needs a name to arrest and Peachun gives him Macheath whom he doesn't know has married his daughter*'.

- The synopsis is completed by a very brief, one sentence, summary of the action, eg

  > '*We follow the villains through their underworld, gangs of car thieves, street criminals and lapdancers in Soho vice clubs as Peachum and Lockit attempt to catch Macheath, who later uncovers Mr Big's pot of gold and turns a policewoman to the dark side.*'

Production details

The writer next focuses on two aspects of the particular production under review. Firstly, she expresses her opinions about the writers of the script (libretto), eg

> '*Nick Dear's script is full of colourful language and references ...*'
> '*He has created a realistic picture that's often not funny but full of irony*'.

She similarly expresses her views on the music (score), eg

> '*I liked Stephen Warbeck's music ...*'
> '*It is a mixture of rock and rock ballads, some using Gay's tunes*'.

Secondly, she comments on the director, eg

> '*Tim Supple, a director known for his innovative, physical productions at the Young Vic and the Royal Shakespeare Company, has created a Mayfair nightclub scene that is so realistic ...*'.

Likewise, she remarks on the set-designer, eg

> '*Robert Innes Hopkins' ten dramatic sets use a backdrop of rolling metal doors, the sky often lit up with local landmarks ...*'.

Thirdly, the writer gives her views on the singing, eg

> '*Madeleine Worrall and Elizabeth Renihan sing well ...*'
> '*Beverley Klein excels as Mrs Peachum belting out her songs ...*'.

Finally, the writer gives an overall assessment of the quality of the production, in which she remarks upon:

- the staging, eg

> '*The final shoot out is well staged, comprehensive and played for laughs.*'

- use of humour, eg

> '*Some of the spoken humour needs local knowledge to be appreciated but the accents are accessible.*'

- the last sentence makes a judgement of the production as a whole, eg

> '*The three hours are well paced, with plenty to laugh at and several tunes one would like to hear again.*'

Written assignment

Write a review of a film, television programme or play with a villainous character that you have watched. Use the information above to help you with the appropriate structure for your review. You should consider:

- context
- synopsis, with setting, characters and their roles, relationships between characters and a one sentence summary of the action
- production details, with script (and music), director and set design/ locations and, if a musical, singing
- overall assessment.

Personal choice

Choose one of the following assignments.

1. Write a personal recount of a villain that you thought was particularly effective in a film, television programme, play or book.
   You should consider:

   - personality
   - behaviour
   - memorable features
   - costume and make-up.

2. Write twenty questions that an interviewer could ask the actor/actress, who is playing the villain, in a current Hollywood action movie.

. . . the shifty villain

The Internet article was originally intended for enthusiasts and professionals, who design 'Dungeons and Dragons' (AD&D) gaming software for computers. The explanation was intended to provide design guidelines for 'Dungeon Masters' (DMs) on how to create 'villains' for the games.

Sometimes we DMs get so busy counting turns, rolling dice, and keeping track of our monsters' hit points and spells that we forget to act, which is a pity, because acting's a big part of the fun of being DM. Some of my favorite times as a DM are when I get to play my favourite – the shifty villain. I love villains.

Major or Minor?

The first thing you have to decide is whether your villain is major or minor. A major villain – an archvillain – is one you're hoping to keep around for a while. A minor villain is just a cameo role, a one-adventure baddie. Major villains need personality and depth. Minor villains are often an instantly recognizable cliché (e.g., the dumb thug, the sleazy weasel, the bragging windbag, the grim killer, the knock 'em dead vamp, the psycho loon).

Nemesis or Hidden Mastermind?

Your major villain is either somebody who will (you hope) plague the characters for levels and levels until The Final Showdown, or somebody who has been operating behind the scenes throughout the campaign and has just been unmasked.

Nemesis: The Nemesis must escape justice every time s/he has a run-in with the adventurers. This is a comic-book cliché but try to keep the Nemesis one step ahead of the characters. If the Nemesis is captured, send the villain to jail. That gives the villain opportunities to escape. Remember, the Nemesis doesn't always need to make a personal appearance. Just a note with the villain's name mentioned in it, a familiar seal on a discarded envelope, or a trademark mutilation on a dead body should be enough.

Hidden Mastermind: The Mastermind is the one who's been behind all the minor villains, the evil genius who has been manipulating the players as though they were pawns on a chess board. You should plan on introducing the Mastermind toward the end. It's best if you make up your mind to include a Mastermind when you first start your planning, because it's easier to weave plots together if you're doing it from the beginning.

First, look at all of your previous adventures and decide how many you can possibly link together. The second step is to start building this information. If you can show how their past actions actually *helped* a criminal in some way, all the better. Once the players realize there's some kind of master plan in the air, they'll start trying to second-guess you. The third step is figuring out the inevitable Unmasking. Who is the Mastermind? Make the Mastermind somebody the characters know and trust. There are two options at this point – make the characters suspect their best friend and find out they're wrong – or find out they're right. A truly nasty Mastermind might frame somebody else, who will only be proven innocent at the last minute. Making the Mastermind somebody the characters love and trust provides the maximum of angst and role-playing opportunity. And remember, the Mastermind is an evil genius. Just because the characters finally realize who it is doesn't mean the Mastermind won't have long since vanished to a secret hideout in preparation for The Final Showdown.

Scum of the Earth or Tragic Antihero?

Is the villain redeemable or irredeemable? Does the villain 'just need killin',' or can s/he be convinced of the evil of his or her ways? Some villains – demons and devils, for example – may be evil because they were created evil and have no free will to change their alignment. To decide whether or not your villain is redeemable, you must first determine the villain's motivation. There are three classic

motivations for villainy: culture, psychology/history, and misguided ideals. All three motivations can lead to the villain either being scum of the earth or a tragic antihero, depending on the villain's personality. Reveal the archvillain's motivations to the characters *before* The Final Showdown. Try to avoid those longwinded James-Bond-movie diatribes from the villain, though. Leave the cheap theatrics for the minor villains. Archvillains should never whine or seek to explain themselves to others. Archvillains have confidence. They're cool. They don't ask permission to be evil. I find redeemable villains to be the most interesting to roleplay: there's far more merit in redeeming the bad guys than in killing them.

Trademarks

Does the villain have a trademark, or is the villain known for being untraceable? The villain with a trademark can be either the Nemesis or the Hidden Mastermind. Trademarks can be left intentionally (riddles, origami birds, a 'Z') or unintentionally (the smell of cigarette smoke, an odd-looking footprint).

The villain who is *perfect* and *never* leaves any clues behind works best as the Hidden Mastermind. The 'perfect' villain usually ends up making a mistake or is betrayed. Does the villain have a fatal flaw that the characters can exploit? (Overconfidence, underconfidence, weakness for the opposite sex, a hot temper.) Does the villain have any likable traits in an otherwise unlikable personality? These and other traits will give the villain some depth. I believe that the best villains are the ones the characters end up liking or admiring despite themselves.

The Final Showdown

The Final Showdown should be the culmination of a series of adventures. Your players want action, drama, and the ever-present threat of death. The ideal Final Showdown is one in which the archvillain knows the characters are coming, and the characters know the archvillain knows, and *both* know that one side or the other isn't going to survive.

The classic Final Showdown occurs in the archvillain's personal stronghold. The archvillain has to be involved in the Final Showdown, but each and every villain or monster who has ever managed to elude the characters or who can be feasibly sprung from jail by the archvillain should be here, ready and waiting. If they specialize in a particular weapon or spell, they should be armed and ready. You wouldn't want to make it easy on the heroes, would you? The archvillain should be around, of course, but s/he shouldn't appear until the characters have been softened up by all the lesser villains, agents, and lackeys.

When the archvillain appears on the scene, the long, winding plotline that has led up to this encounter is finally coming to an end. Once the archvillain has either been captured, killed, or has undergone a change of heart, the characters will probably collect their booty and drag their dead, dying, and walking wounded out of the dungeon. This is the decompression stage, and it's best not to throw anything more at the characters. There's little point in staging any important scenes after The Final Showdown – they'll detract from the moment and after this game, you're going to have to figure out what to run *next* ... and The Final Showdown with the campaign's archvillain is a tough act to follow!

TEXT LEVEL WORK

Comprehension

A 1 What is a DM?

2 What does the writer say is his favourite time as a DM?

3 What is an archvillain?

4 What is the Final Showdown?

5 Where does the classic Final Showdown occur?

B 1 Explain, in your own words, what is meant by the following:

　a '*a one-adventure baddie*'
　b '*to weave plots together*'
　c '*scum of the earth*'
　d '*cheap theatrics*'.

2 What do you think the writer means by an '*instantly recognizable cliché*'?

3 What do you think are the first two important decisions that have to be made about a villain?

4 What do you think the writer means by the '*trademarks of a villain*'?

C 1 Explain what you see as the main differences between a '*Nemesis*' and a '*Hidden Mastermind*'.

2 Explain what you think the writer had in mind when he asked the question, '*Scum of the Earth or Tragic Antihero?*'

WORD LEVEL WORK

Vocabulary

Dictionary and contextual work
Use a dictionary and the context of the passage to explain the meanings of the following words:

1 software	5 psycho	9 genius
2 lackeys	6 campaign	10 nemesis
3 cameo	7 cliché	11 redeemable
4 vamp	8 mutilation	12 angst

Spelling

'ch' saying hard 'c'
Key words: **ch**aracters　　psy**ch**ology

1 Use these key words in sentences of your own.

2 Learn these important 'ch' words:

　stoma**ch**　　**ch**orus　　**ch**oir　　**ch**ronology

　or**ch**estra　　**ch**emical　　**ch**ord

SENTENCE LEVEL WORK

Grammar and punctuation

Paragraphs – indicating sequence in non-fiction writing to explain

> Remember. A *paragraph* is a group of related sentences focusing on one topic beginning with a *topic sentence.* The initial idea from the topic sentence is expanded, giving more detail, information or examples. Writers make use of *headings* and *sub-headings*, eg
>
> **'Trademarks'**
>
> Headings and sub-headings use different fonts, sizes or formatting, such as italics or underlining. Writers may also choose words that show the sequence of the explanation, eg
>
> *'First'*

Copy and complete the table. In each row, under the appropriate heading, write the reason why you think the indicator is a heading, sub-heading or sequence word/phrase.

	Heading	Sub-heading	Sequence
Nemesis			
Scum of the Earth or Tragic Antihero?			
The second step			
The Final Showdown			
When			
Hidden Mastermind			
The third step			
Nemesis or Hidden Mastermind?			
Sometimes			
Once			
The first thing			
Major or Minor?			

TEXT LEVEL WORK

Writing

Advice and guidance

> The Internet article was originally intended for enthusiasts and professionals, who design 'Dungeons and Dragons' (AD&D) gaming software for computers. The explanation provides design guidelines for 'Dungeon Masters' (DMs) on how to create 'villains' for the games. The writer begins with an introduction, before laying out the rest in sections, using headings and sub-headings. The guidelines follow a logical series of steps, using imperative verb tenses.

Language features

Structuring writing – introduction

The introduction is a straight-forward personal statement, by the writer, eg

'... acting's a big part of the fun of being DM ...'
'Some of my favourite times as a DM are when I get to play my favourite – the shifty villain. I love villains.'

This interests the reader, introducing the subject.

Questions and answers

The writer uses questions a great deal, in the passage, eg

'Is the villain redeemable or irredeemable?'

He then answers the questions and, by doing so, gives the reader advice, eg

'To decide whether or not your villain is redeemable, you must first determine the villain's motivation.'

The writer then expands the guidance in more detail, eg

'There are three classic motivations for villainy ...'.

Next, the writer offers advice on how to deal with the challenge raised by the initial question, eg

'Reveal the archvillain's motivations to the characters before The Final Showdown.'

Sequencing

In structuring the advice, the writer develops the villain logically in the phrasing used, eg

'First ...'   'The second step is ...'   'The third step is ...'
'There are two options at this point ...'.

Imperative verbs

The writer uses imperative verbs when emphasising certain steps in the development of the villains, eg

'Make ...'   'Reveal ...'   'Try to ...'.

Person

The writer uses the first person to stress their personal advice, eg

'I believe ...'   'I find ...'.

The writer uses the second person when asking rhetorical questions, which do not expect an answer, eg

'You wouldn't want to make it easy on the heroes, would you?'

Writing assignment

Write a set of guidelines, giving advice to an actor/actress, who is to play a villain, in a forthcoming film. You should include:

- relationships with other characters
- facial expressions
- style of movements/mannerisms
- tones of voice and style of language
- costume and make-up.

In your explanation, you should consider:

- questions and answers that you need to draw attention to
- sequencing
- use of the imperative
- use of the first and second person.

Personal choice

Choose one of the following assignments.

1 Research and make notes on villains, such as Bill Sykes in *Oliver Twist*, Iago in *Othello* or Edward Hyde in *Dr Jekyll and Mr Hyde*. Write an explanation of how they are villainous.

2 Write a short story, in which an archvillain pits his wits against a hero.

...unnatural malice.

To Prove a Villain – The Elizabethan Villain as Revenger

Revenge is a kind of wild justice, which the more man's nature runs to, the more ought law to weed it out; for as for the first wrong, it doth but offend the law, but the revenge of that wrong putteth the law out of office.

(Bacon, Sir Francis. *An Anthology of English Classics.* New York: Rinehart & Company, 1935.)

A villain is a person who, for a selfish end, wilfully and deliberately violates the standards of morality sanctioned by the audience or reader. From the start, the Elizabethan villain had been entirely self-conscious, and entirely black, a complete embodiment of evil. With the growing consciousness that revenge was evil, revengefulness – particularly for injuries less than blood – became almost exclusively a villainous characteristic. Revenge is not a Christian attribute. Christian virtue, with its great emphasis on forgiveness, is a higher mode of behaviour than pagan revenge. As Prospero observes in William Shakespeare's *The Tempest*, forgiveness is a nobler action than vengeance.

For the Elizabethans the villain could have many motives that would be cause for revenge: anger, jealousy, and envy. Anger is most often the motive with hatred a close second. Hatred, in the eyes of another, was defined as natural wrath which had endured too long and had turned to unnatural malice. Anger (or choler) comes from personal wrongs, it is felt for particular men as opposed to hatred which is felt for all humanity. Anger can be cured by patience, but hatred is everlasting. Anger wants the victim to recognize the revenger, whereas hatred only desires to watch the destruction of the victim without recognition. Jealousy is another prime motive of revenge, it stems from the belief that an adversary or rival is an obstacle, that this adversary may hinder or cross the design and purpose of the revenger. Envy was considered the greatest Elizabethan vice, and it may be one of the most powerful of the passions inducing revenge. Envy's passion was so great that, in contrast to anger, no wrongs were necessary for a person to become the recipient of its malice; indeed, it was often directed against the most virtuous and peaceful of men.

The Merchant of Venice by Shakespeare, remains as compelling today as it was four centuries ago, because it comments so eloquently on a universal theme, the drive for revenge. *The Merchant of Venice* is exceptional among Shakespeare's plays because it may have been inspired, at least indirectly, by a contemporary scandal. In 1594 the Queen's personal physician Roderigo Lopez, a Portuguese Jew, was tried and executed for treason. The Lopez case inspired a wave of anti-Jewish feeling, and was probably responsible for the appearance of several dramas dealing with Jewish characters, including a revival of *The Jew of Malta*. If the Lopez affair did serve as Shakespeare's inspiration, only a few hints of this remain in the text of *The Merchant of Venice*. (One of these is that the hero of the play may be named for Don Antonio, the pretender to the Portuguese throne, who was associated with Dr. Lopez). In Shakespeare's hands, the Jewish villain became a complex character whose drive for revenge many playgoers can understand and even sympathize with. The elements of treachery and suspense are balanced with light hearted romance to create a drama which many audiences find more satisfying than Shakespeare's farcical early comedies.

The English of the late sixteenth century believed that Christianity was the only true religion, and that the social order was ordained by God. The individual who set himself against the establishment could only be a source of disruption or, at worst, evil. Since Jews did not believe in Christianity, they were a threat to the social order. The character of Shylock in *The Merchant of Venice* was no doubt drawn from literature, not real life. The Jewish villain was a stock character in medieval literature. Medieval passion plays, reenactments of the story of the crucifixion of Jesus, invariably portrayed the disloyal disciple Judas, as a stereotypical Jew. (Of course, historically, Jesus and all of his disciples were Jewish, but this was ignored.) The part of Judas was usually

played for comedy, by an actor wearing an outrageous red wig and a large false nose. Subsequent authors, when they portrayed Jewish characters, always cast them as villains. In all probability, Shakespeare was not even interested in Shylock's Jewishness. He used the prevailing anti-Semitic stereotypes as a handy way to characterize his play's villain. Barabas, *The Jew of Malta*, must have been the prototype for Shylock. What mattered to Shakespeare was that Shylock was an outsider set apart from society because of his religion, his profession of lending money for interest, and his hatred for Antonio and the other Christian characters of the play. Surely Shylock wouldn't take the pound of flesh even if Antonio did fail to pay his loan, Salerio says: "What's that good for?" "If it will feed nothing else, it will feed my revenge." Shylock answers (3.1.47–49). Shylock has no interest in money, he wants revenge for the way he had been abused – and if the loss of a pound of flesh costs Antonio his life, so much the better.

Villains were equipped with motives other than just pure revengefulness. Covetness, misanthropy, and especially ambition, often hold the stage almost unchallenged. The ambitious villain has a love of conquest and a thirst for power. Sometimes the ambitious villain can be thought of as a revengeful villain. In Christopher Marlowe's *The Jew of Malta*, Barabas was by nature ambitious, but most of his actions were the result of a desire for revenge. Barabas, describes his character to the audience thus:

Now will I show myself to have more of the serpent than the dove; that is, more knave than fool. (*The Jew of Malta*, 2.3.36–37)

His enemies blocked his ambition, so he turned to retaliation.

In Marlowe's play, which was first performed in 1591, Barabas is a very wealthy Jewish merchant who lives on the Mediterranean island of Malta. Like Shylock, Barabas has an only daughter who is in love with a Christian. Barabas also has a rational motive for hating Christian society. In the play, he is angered by the passage of a law requiring all Jews to either convert to Christianity or give up one half of their wealth. Nevertheless, Barabas is a thoroughly evil character. Barabas possesses great wealth and uses it in such a manner as to make him more powerful than kings. He commits crimes for revenge, because he hates Christians as such, and hates especially the men who have taken his gold. He resorts to murder and treason to gain his revenge and enjoys watching the pain and suffering he has caused.

TEXT LEVEL WORK

Comprehension

A 1 In which of Shakespeare's plays does the character of Prospero appear?

2 Who was Queen Elizabeth's doctor?

3 In which year was the Queen's doctor tried and executed?

4 For what crime was the doctor tried and executed?

5 In which of Shakespeare's plays does the character of Shylock appear?

B 1 What was funny about the character of Judas, in the medieval passion plays?

2 Who was the author, and what was the play, in which Barabas appears?

3 The Elizabethans believed that villains could have many motives: name three.

4 Explain the following in your own words:

   a '*a rational motive*'

   b '*contemporary scandal*'

   c '*unnatural malice*'.

C 1 What evidence is there in the passage that the writer thinks that Shakespeare was not even interested in Shylock's Jewishness? Quote in support of your answer.

2 To what extent might Shakespeare's character of Shylock be based on Marlowe's Barabas? Give evidence to support your answer.

WORD LEVEL WORK

Vocabulary

Dictionary and contextual work

Use a dictionary and the context of the passage to explain the meanings of the following words:

1 revenge	4 embodiment	7 wrath	10 malice
2 villain	5 attribute	8 adversary	11 virtuous
3 morality	6 pagan	9 recipient	12 eloquently

Spelling

'or' words

Key words: p**or**trayed   rec**or**ds   hist**or**y   act**or**

1 Use these key words in sentences of your own.

2 Learn these important 'or' words:

   direct**or**   narrat**or**   auth**or**   maj**or**

   min**or**   trait**or**   curs**or**

SENTENCE LEVEL WORK

Grammar and punctuation

Sentence construction – clause conjunctions

Remember. Many sentences contain more than one clause. Clauses are joined together by *conjunctions*. There must be a relationship of meaning between the clauses. The conjunction used to join the clauses must be suitable for the relationship of meaning between the clauses. Clauses may:

- be related by the idea of time, using conjunctions, eg

   'before', 'after', 'during', 'since', 'while', 'when'

- add an idea to another clause, joined using conjunctions, eg

   'and', 'in addition', 'also', 'plus', 'furthermore', 'moreover'.

Conjunctions may:

- indicate that one clause is used to emphasise the other clause, eg
    'indeed', 'in fact'
- show that the two clauses demonstrate differences and should suggest the negative – think of it as 'NOT', eg
    'however', 'nevertheless', 'but', 'although', 'yet'
- come either at the beginning of a sentence, or in the middle of a sentence.

Where the action of one clause only happens because of the other clause, this is called *condition*. In this case, the conjunction used is 'if'.

Where one clause may cause another, this is called *causality*, and the conjunctions needed include 'because', 'consequently', 'for', 'since', 'therefore'.

Copy and complete the table. Circle the conjunctions that are used to join the clauses. Write what type of relationship exists between the clauses: time, condition, causality, not, emphasis or addition.

Sentence	Relationship
Since Jews did not believe in Christianity, they were a threat to the social order.	
Barabas also has a rational motive for hating Christian society.	
"If it will feed nothing else, it will feed my revenge."	
The Merchant of Venice by Shakespeare, remains as compelling today as it was four centuries ago, because it comments so eloquently on a universal theme, the drive for revenge.	
Envy's passion was so great that, in contrast to anger, no wrongs were necessary for a person to become the recipient of its malice; indeed, it was often directed against the most virtuous and peaceful of men.	
Anger wants the victim to recognize the revenger, whereas hatred only desires to watch the destruction of the victim without recognition.	

TEXT LEVEL WORK

Writing

Writing to inform

The passage gives the reader information about the desire for revenge in the Elizabethan villains. It begins with a definition of a villain in the context of the Elizabethan period. The writer examines the motives of villains such as Shylock.

Language features

Formal language – sentence construction

The writer is formal in his use of language, so sentences are complicated, eg

> 'Envy's passion was so great that, in contrast to anger, no wrongs were necessary for a person to become the recipient of its malice; indeed, it was often directed against the most virtuous and peaceful of men.'

The writer uses full sentences without unnecessary detail, eg

> 'Revenge is not a Christian attribute.'

Formal language will often avoid using contractions, eg

> 'Revenge is not ...' is used instead of 'Revenge isn't ...'.

Passive voice

Formal language often uses the passive voice, eg

> 'The English of the late sixteenth century believed that Christianity was the only true religion, and that the social order was ordained by God.'

Vocabulary

The passage contains vocabulary specific to the Elizabethan villain, eg

> 'As Prospero observes in William Shakespeare's The Tempest, forgiveness is a nobler action than vengeance.'

Quotations

The writer uses quotations to support the information, eg

> 'Now will I show myself to have more of the serpent than the dove; that is, more knave than fool. (The Jew of Malta, 2.3.36–37)'.

Opinion and fact

The writer reduces opinion and concentrates on the facts, eg

> 'In Marlowe's play, which was first performed in 1591, Barabas is a very wealthy Jewish merchant who lives on the Mediterranean island of Malta.'

Factual information is grouped into topics related by their subject with a topic sentence:

> 'For the Elizabethans the villain could have many motives that would be cause for revenge: anger, jealousy, and envy.'

The remainder of the paragraph explores the topic, eg

> 'Anger is most often the motive ...'
> 'Jealousy is another prime motive ...'
> 'Envy was considered ...'.

Writing assignment

Look back over the three units of work concerned with villains, in this book. Using the information and language features above, write an assignment that provides information about a typical 'hero'. You should consider:

- sentence constructions
- passive voice
- vocabulary
- quotations
- facts.

Personal choice

Choose one of the following assignments.

1 Pick one hero from film, television, a play or a book, and describe how they are heroic.

2 Write a personal recount of somebody that you considered to be 'your hero'. Give full explanations about why you think of them as a hero.

Published in 2003 by:
Nelson Thornes Ltd
Delta Place
27 Bath Road
CHELTENHAM
GL53 7TH
United Kingdom

12 / 10 9 8

A catalogue record for this book is available from the British Library

ISBN 978 0 7487 6948 3

Illustration by Martin Berry, Zhenya Matysiak, The Richardson Studio
Designed by Viners Wood Associates

Printed in China

Acknowledgements
The authors and publishers are grateful to the following for permission to reproduce copyright material and photographs for this book:

BBC Worldwide for material from David McNab and James Younger, The Planets (1999). Copyright © David McNab and James Younger 1999; Garth Haslam material from his article, 'The Cottingley Fairies'. Copyright © 2002 Garth Haslam; Hodder and Stoughton Ltd for material from Jim Lovell and Jeffrey Kluger, Apollo 13 (1995) pp. 101-4; Independent Newspapers (UK) Ltd for Stephen Goodwin, 'Return of death penalty rejected', The Independent, 22.2.94; The New York Times for material from William J Broad, 'Scientists Close in on Elusive Giant Squid', The New York Times, 13.2.96. Copyright © 1996 by the New York Times Co.; Times Newspapers Ltd for material from instructions, 'How to explore your CD-Rom', The Sunday Times Magazine, 23.9.01. Copyright © 2001 Times Newspapers Ltd; and Brian Sibley, 'Fantasy Made Flesh', The Sunday Times Magazine, 25.11.01. Copyright © 2001 Times Newspapers Ltd; The Washington Post Writers Group for Guy Gugliotta, 'Black Sea Artifacts May Be Evidence of Biblical Flood', The Washington Post, 13.9.00. Copyright © 2000 The Washington Post; Zambia National Tourist Board for material from their website.

Mary Evans Picture Library, pp. 4, 58; Camera Press, p. 10; Ronald Grant, front cover, pp. 16, 64; Science Photo Library, back cover, pp. 22, 23, 46; Famous, p. 28; Digital Vision 9 (NT), p. 34; © Anglo-Australian Obs./Royal Obs. Edinburgh, p. 35; Images of Africa, back cover, p. 40; Corel 800 (NT), p. 76; Corel 650 (NT), p. 82; Corel 11 (NT), p. 88; London Stills.com, p. 94; Digital Vision 5 (NT), p. 100; Donald Cooper/Photostage, p. 106.

Every effort has been made to trace the copyright holders but if any have been inadvertently overlooked the publishers will be pleased to make the necessary arrangement at the first opportunity.